Praise for *Five Minutes on Mondays*

"*Five Minutes on Mondays*" is a gold mine of enrichment for both the soul and the new bottom line. It is an easy read with a deep and profound impact. Start your work week by reading a chapter every Monday, and you'll stay fulfilled all the way to Friday."

—**Martin Rutte**, Chair of the Board, The Centre for Spirituality and the Workplace, Saint Mary's University, and co-author of the *New York Times* business best-seller, *Chicken Soup for the Soul at Work*

"*Five Minutes on Mondays* is one of those breakthrough books that one can't help giving to every corporate nay-sayer you know. Full of uncommon wisdom that we sometimes miss in everyday life, it's a beautifully written near-manifesto about making work life a lot more fruitful."

—**Charles Decker**, publishing consultant and author of *Lessons from the Hive: The Buzz on Surviving and Thriving in an Ever-Changing Workplace*

"I began to read this book at the end of a stressful day. About 30 pages in I realized that the stress had faded and in its place was a quiet peacefulness. I found this remarkable. I believe you will, too. Highly recommended."

—**Stewart Emery**, best-selling co-author of *Success Built to Last* and *Do You Matter?*

"Lurie's wise and wonderful book should grace every karmic capitalist's bookshelf. His clever and deep thoughts underline the fact that devotion isn't purely limited to the spiritual world, nor is the idea of being successful purely a concept for those working in skyscrapers. Alan reminds us that finding a sense of meaning and purpose in what we do may align us with unimagined success and a profound awakening to who we are."

—**Chip Conley**, CEO, Joie de Vivre Hotels

"Most collections of business aphorisms instruct us on 'what to do' to be successful. Alan Lurie operates on a different level and is suggesting 'who to be' to be successful. In this book, Alan is pointing to a way of 'Being' that honors the human spirit. Read Alan's suggestions to elevate your spirit—then bring that spirit to your work. The promise is: both you and your client will be more fulfilled, more satisfied, and more engaged in your business relationship."

—**John King**, Senior Partner, CultureSync, and co-author of *Tribal Leadership*

FIVE MINUTES
ON MONDAYS

FIVE MINUTES ON MONDAYS

FINDING UNEXPECTED PURPOSE, PEACE, AND FULFILLMENT AT WORK

ALAN LURIE

Vice President, Publisher: Tim Moore
Associate Publisher and Director of Marketing: Amy Neidlinger
Editorial Assistant: Pamela Boland
Development Editor: Russ Hall
Operations Manager: Gina Kanouse
Digital Marketing Manager: Julie Phifer
Publicity Manager: Laura Czaja
Assistant Marketing Manager: Megan Colvin
Cover Designer: Chuti Prasertsith
Managing Editor: Kristy Hart
Project Editor: Chelsey Marti
Copy Editor: Water Crest Publishing, Inc.
Proofreader: Language Logistics, LLC; Williams Woods Publishing, LLC
Indexer: Erika Millen
Compositor: Bronkella Publishing, LLC
Manufacturing Buyer: Dan Uhrig

FT Press offers excellent discounts on this book when ordered in quantity for bulk purchases or special sales. For more information, please contact U.S. Corporate and Government Sales, 1-800-382-3419, corpsales@pearsontechgroup.com. For sales outside the U.S., please contact International Sales at international@pearson.com.

First Printing March 2009

ISBN-10: 0-13-700778-7
ISBN-13: 978-0-13-700778-3

Pearson Education LTD.
Pearson Education Australia PTY, Limited.
Pearson Education Singapore, Pte. Ltd.
Pearson Education North Asia, Ltd.
Pearson Education Canada, Ltd.
Pearson Educación de Mexico, S.A. de C.V.
Pearson Education—Japan
Pearson Education Malaysia, Pte. Ltd.

Library of Congress Cataloging-in-Publication Data

Lurie, Alan J., 1958-
   Five minutes on Mondays : finding unexpected purpose, peace, and fulfillment at work / Alan Lurie.
        p. cm.
   ISBN 0-13-700778-7 (hardback : alk. paper) 1. Work ethic. 2.   Work--
Psychological aspects. 3.   Chance. 4.   Self-actualization (Psychology) 5.   Peace of
mind--Religious aspects. I. Title. II. Title: Inner peace and self- fulfillment at work.
   HD4905.L87 2009
   650.1--dc22
                            2008036457

To those who dream of, work for, and struggle with, the promise of heaven on earth.

CONTENTS

ACKNOWLEDGMENTS

T heologians define grace as:

The free and unmerited favor or beneficence of God.

Grace is experienced when we receive an unexpected gift that was given to us simply because the giver desires to give. For me, this book has truly been a gift of grace, steered by many extraordinary people who graciously gave their time, attention, support, and guidance. I am very grateful to many such people.

First, I thank my wife, Shirona, who has been given many great gifts: a magnificent voice, artistic talent, spiritual intuition, and the drive to manifest beauty. She has taken the Biblical injunction that a wife should be a "helper who challenges him [her husband]" to heart, and much of the content in this book is a result of her insights, as well as her challenge that I speak and write with authenticity and humility.

Second, I owe much to my children, Will and David, who awakened the father in me, and who continually keep me grounded. I also thank my parents, Arnold and Flora, who have always maintained their love and support as they watched me struggle to find my way.

I thank my teacher and guide, Rabbi Joseph Gelberman. His life is a model of a commitment to kindness and wisdom, and he is an inspiration to countless students, congregants, and the fortunate stranger who wanders his way. May he live to 120 in good health!

This book would not ever have come into existence without the vision of my friend and mentor David Arena, President of Grubb & Ellis, who shows that the principles in this book are not theoretical. He walks the talk of the spiritual businessman. I also thank the New York staff of Grubb & Ellis, who took valuable time from their busy day to listen to my words. I hope that, in some way, their investment paid off.

My thanks to Martin Rutte, who took me under his wing, and graciously opened a door that I did not know existed.

I am grateful to my friends, colleagues, teachers, students, and clients, who are often the characters and inspiration for the stories, experiences, and lessons captured in this book.

Finally, I thank my publishers, Stewart Emery and Tim Moore, who saw in me a kindred spirit, and in this book something worth communicating to a larger audience.

About the Author

Alan Lurie has a unique background. He is currently a Managing Director at Grubb & Ellis, a national real estate service firm, following a 25-year career as a licensed architect. He is also a non-denominational ordained Rabbi, teaching, leading prayer services, and writing on issues of faith and religion. This combination of meeting the demands of the business world while attending to the needs of the spirit gives Alan both insight into, and access to, a diverse community. His wife, Shirona, is a Jewish Cantor, singer, and accomplished songwriter. They live in Rye, New York.

INTRODUCTION

As we look back on the arc of our lives, we often discover that the most significant, meaningful changes came from unexpected, seemingly unremarkable, or even un-welcomed sources. While we were busy planning the direction in which we thought our lives should go, something unplanned entered to steer us onto a new path that led to a destination that we could not possibly have imagined. Something that at first seemed to be a distraction, nuisance, or, perhaps, an outright disaster was, in retrospect, the best thing that could have happened. It shook us out of our routine, allowed for new possibilities to enter, and presented the opportunity to rise above our previous sense of how things should be, what we are capable of doing, and who we are. We now realize that without these uninvited events, we would have gone along on our regular, tired path, and none of these changes would have happened.

These events are gifts of grace, and whether we recognize them and decide to listen to their call or to reject these gifts, we are all helped along and redirected in this way. The creation of this book traveled just such a path, and came about through a series of events and encounters with extraordinary people that I could not possibly have conceived of, and to whom I am very grateful. The unlikely ingredients in the recipe of events from which this book emerged include a commuter train, a sweltering August day in New York City, a sweaty business card, recurring random encounters, and a spilled beer. Through these events I met David Arena, President of Grubb & Ellis—a national commercial real estate firm.

Buddhism teaches that we should embrace awkwardness; that this feeling is a signal that we are on the right path toward growth. By embracing awkwardness, we begin to drop the ego's desire to project an image that defends us from experiencing our true, tender selves. We might think that others are impressed when we appear sophisticated, professional, witty, cool, or clever, but this teaching reminds us that we are most impressive when we are authentic. The events surrounding this book have helped to teach me the truth of this ancient wisdom.

David and I first met on a hot and humid day in August on the Metro-North commuter train, which travels from Grand Central Station to Connecticut. I had just run 20 blocks to catch the 6:15 train and slipped in as the doors were closing. Sitting across from me was a man whose face I recognized from a recent cover of *Crain's Business Journal*.

That's David Arena! I should introduce myself, I thought, *but look at me. I'm drenched.... Hey, what's the worst that can happen?*

So, I leaned over to introduce myself. With sweat dripping from my forehead, I reached in to my pocket and pulled out a soggy, limp business card, which he politely accepted, then returned to reading his newspaper.

That certainly went well, Lurie, I thought, assuming I had just blown a promising business opportunity.

Several months later, we ran into each other again. This was on a Friday afternoon, as I was sitting on the train studying a Hebrew text and drinking a beer (two things that I like to do as I head home for the weekend). I looked up to see David sit down next to me. He glanced at my book and, apparently not remembering that we had met, said,

"Excuse me. Is that Hebrew?"

"Yes. It's actually a section from the Bible."

"Really? Are you a religious man?" he asked.

"As a matter of fact, I'm an ordained Rabbi," I answered, "but I also work in commercial real estate. We actually met briefly on this train last summer, and I gave you my card."

We struck up a conversation, and discovered a shared interest in religion and theology (a conversation that he later described as "being kinda' out there"). As I got up to leave, I bent over to shake his hand and accidentally spilled beer on his sleeve and into his briefcase.

"Now I've been baptized by a Rabbi," he laughed.

I walked off the train, wondering how I could have been so clumsy, and why I seemed to keep spilling things on this man.

The third time I saw David was in a midtown office reception area. I had taken the day off to do some work around the house but came by this office to drop off a package. Unshaved, uncombed, and dressed in worn jeans and a tee shirt, I turned to see David walk in.

This makes sense, I thought. *God forbid I should run into him looking professional!*

"Good to see you again, Rabbi," he said, patting me on the back. "Let's meet for breakfast soon. Here's my card. Please call me."

"Why do you think I keep meeting this man under such awkward circumstances?" I later asked my wife, Shirona. "The first time we met, I looked like I had just run a marathon in a business suit. The second time, I spilled beer all over him, and the third time, I could have been mistaken for the delivery man."

"Don't worry," she said, "At least he's going to remember you! I think there's more to this than just random encounters, though."

After this, David and I continued to run into each other on numerous occasions—on the street, in offices, at industry events, and on the train, and we soon became friends. Then, unexpectedly, he asked me to join his team at Grubb & Ellis. (Now, after two years of working together, I have only seen him on the train twice.)

"I've got to tell you, it's not often that a stranger on a train hands me a sweaty business card, discusses mystical ideas about the nature of the cosmos, and then pours beer in my briefcase. You definitely made a unique impression," he said, then added, "I believe that this will be a good place for you, Alan. With us, you'll have the opportunity to do good work, both in your profession as a businessman and your passion as a Rabbi. Look, I have an idea. Our entire group meets every Monday morning at 8:00 AM, and I'd like you to begin these meetings by delivering a short message. Something about business and ethics. Something inspirational and informative."

This was certainly a novel idea. A Rabbi/businessman delivering a sermon to a New York City real estate meeting! David had never heard me speak in public, and didn't ask to review what I was going to say, yet he somehow had the faith that this would work. Initially, I was not so confident.

And so, on one Monday morning in January 2007, I awkwardly stood in front of 100 or so hard-nosed New York real estate professionals to deliver my first message. I had searched for something to talk about that I hoped would be interesting, useful, inspiring, and entertaining to a business community whose reputation is not exactly toward things spiritual. This first message was titled "Donkey for Sale."

(Well, you'll have to read it to get the reference!) In it, I said, "There are many who immediately link business and money to dishonesty, greed, and sin. Is this just the way it is, though?" I asked. "Is there a way to experience success in business, to be comfortable, even wealthy, and to live a life committed to honesty and to the "golden rule" of treating others with respect and love?"

I explained that, "In Hebrew, the word for *work* is *avodah*, which also, surprisingly, means *prayer*. This teaches us that there is a direct connection between the physical world of work and the nonphysical world of the spirit. Both are seen as instruments of personal and social change which, when operated in harmony, reinforce each other. Just as we pray for the blessings of spiritual sustenance, we work for the blessings of physical sustenance. The connection of these words creates an understanding that work must be approached with the same reverence that we give to prayer (and, conversely, that prayer requires work, commitment, dedication, and regular practice). In this model, success at work is a blessing that eases our lives and supports and enriches those around us. This model states that, just as the world, if treated with respect, is filled with endless abundance, when work is approached with reverence there is more than enough for all. Spiritual business is based on the premise that, contrary to the common paradigm, one person's gain need not be another's loss; that success and abundance for one does not create scarcity for others."

After this, I delivered messages almost every week. In addition to reading the messages to the Grubb & Ellis team, I also wrote them down to e-mail to the staff, as well as to colleagues, clients, and friends This book captures a selection of these weekly messages delivered over the course of one year, along with a few additional complimentary essays and speeches given in other venues during that time.

The messages focus on many of the common issues that most of us struggle with: How can I more effectively understand others and be understood? How can I prosper financially while maintaining my integrity? When should I say what's on my mind, and when should I let it go? How can I keep going and maintain optimism in the face of challenges and setbacks? Is it possible to balance all the demands on my time and energy? Where can I find a sense of meaning and purpose? None of these questions is new, and a vast body of philosophy, psychology, sociology, and theology has provided insightful and useful answers. These messages draw on a wide variety of these sources, but from several uncommon perspectives.

First, the primary intent of these messages is to show that the highest teachings from all these traditions ultimately point toward the same direction, which is, simply stated, the path to becoming better human beings; more caring about others, more intellectually engaged, more connected to our bodies, and more fully awake to the flow of our lives. The principles and practices that these traditions teach foster positive growth in all these aspects of our lives, leading to success and satisfaction at work; meaningful relationships with our friends, family, and community; good physical health; a clearer vision of our truest selves; and a deeper soul connection to the Divine. Although we may tend to view these as separate endeavors, the greatest teachings from all significant traditions tell us that this image of separateness is a harmful illusion, and that we function at our fullest, healthiest, and highest potential when all these aspects operate in unity.

The second uncommon perspective is embedded in the context of these messages: They were prepared for the business community, and usually stem from observations or events that happened at work. These messages propose that the daily activities at work create a perfect "spiritual gymnasium," where we are faced with very real dilemmas and interactions that require a very real response. Theology and philosophy may propose beautiful ideals, and we may think that spirituality is found only in prayer, religious text study, or on the meditation pillow, but the rubber hits the road when we are faced with implementing these ideals in the complex world of work. If we are committed to true, meaningful growth, then, work is a deeply spiritual environment where, through our actions, we can implement our obligations to others, build our confidence and sense of purpose, practice our commitment to the truth, strengthen our inherent optimism, experience gratitude, and live with a greater sense of balance.

The Rabbis of the Talmud—the Jewish compendium of ethical debate—wonder, "What is the first question that one is asked when standing in front of the heavenly court?" In other words, what's the most important question that determines whether you lived a good life? They decide that, ahead of the questions, "Did you study?," "Did you pray?," or "Did you give to charity?," is the question, "Did you conduct your business affairs honestly?" The Rabbis recognize that business success is a powerful goal, and that one can be easily tempted to do "whatever it takes" to succeed. The person who can resist these temptations and conduct business in an honest fashion, though, has truly lived according to the highest standard. So, do you still think that your job is not spiritual?

The third uncommon perspective is mentioned at the beginning of this Introduction and alluded to throughout the following messages: uncertainty as a gateway to growth. We live in times of uncertainty and enormous, rapid change. This uncertainty may be frightening. It may be intimidating. It is definitely unsettling. We may wish that things could stay put, and may feel a desire for solid, familiar ground. But, the messages in this book propose that we view uncertainty in a different way. Uncertainty can, in fact, be a great gift, because it can cause us to re-think our established, fixed way of seeing things, and help the transformation from stagnation to move-ment; from limitation to expansion. This process leads to change and growth, which is the basis of all life. Without change and growth, our mind, body, emotions, and spirit begin to atrophy, solidify, and decay. As Benjamin Franklin succinctly wrote:

When you're finished changing, you're finished.

Uncertainty and change expose the hidden defenses that we've created to protect us from revealing our insecurities, and once exposed, these defenses begin to weaken. Then, if we are willing, we can walk through a new door that opens to the untold, unimaginable potential that is our birthright as human beings.

In the following messages, I have tried to touch on these three perspectives:

1. Find unity.
2. Practice spiritual growth through work.
3. Embrace uncertainty.

These can be very difficult to implement. I know because I struggle with them daily. I hope, though, that this struggle has resulted in some insights that are elevating, useful, and enjoyable.

Wishing you well,

Alan Lurie
June 2008

DONKEY FOR SALE

ETHICAL WEALTH

There are many well-known and funny oxy-morons—phrases that are internally self-contradictory—such as the following:

- Civil war
- Forward retreat
- Fresh frozen
- Jumbo shrimp
- Light heavyweight
- Negative growth

How about an honest businessperson? Or a wealthy spiritual person? To many, these are clearly contradictory. This is because we might have been told that to succeed in business, we have to bend the rules, engage in dishonest activities, and play dirty. We may also believe that religion and spirituality disdain monetary wealth, or that a person dedicated to spiritual pursuits cannot succeed in the brutal business arena. Such a person, we may think, will get stuck on the rungs of the ladder to success at the first inevitable call to dishonesty. We may hear such a person say, "My commitment to honesty shut me out of the executive suite," or "I could have made a lot of money, but I wasn't willing to sell my soul!"

We might have been told that to succeed in business, we have to bend the rules, engage in dishonest activities, and play dirty.

There certainly are many who immediately link business and money to dishonesty, greed, and sin. Is this just the way it is, though? Is there a way to experience success in business, to be comfortable, even wealthy, and to live a life committed to honesty and to the "golden rule" of treating others with respect and love? There are two wonderful Yiddish sayings that address these questions in the typical Yiddish manner—head on, with irony and humor.

One:

It's not that having money is so good: It's that not having money is so bad.

The other:

I have been rich, and I have been poor—and I can tell you it is better to be rich and happy than poor and miserable.

And then, of course, there is Tevya, the poor dairyman in *Fiddler on the Roof*, who complains to the heavens:

I know there is no shame in being poor, but it's no great honor either.

These are funny because they are so obvious. Of course it's good to have money, to be comfortable, or, at least, to not be poor. But these sayings also allude to a deeper truth. Although the path to business success for some may be littered with cheating, lying, gossiping, and plain old corruption, we all must know that those who achieve success through this route are not, in the long run, honorable or happy; not truly "honorable" or "happy" in the deepest sense of the words—as someone who lives with a meaningful purpose, in meaningful connection to others, and to the finest that is within. That is because no matter how deeply one buries one's conscience, the voice of morality, which is intrinsically embedded in all of us, will be heard.

There is an illuminating argument written in the Talmud—the Jewish record of ethical and legal discussions—that emphasizes this point. In this debate, the Rabbis wonder, "What is the first question that one is asked when standing in front of the heavenly court?" In other words, what's the most important question that determines how well you lived your life? Behind the scenes, the Rabbis argue; one says that the first question must be, "Did you pray every day?" Another asserts that it is, "Did you study?" And another, "Did you give money to charity?" Finally, one suggests, "Did you conduct your business affairs honestly?" Immediately all agree that this is the correct first question. The Rabbis recognize that, although the other activities are absolutely essential, business success is such a powerful goal that one can be easily tempted to do "whatever it takes" to succeed. The person who can resist these temptations and conduct business in an honest fashion, though, has truly lived according to the highest standard. This person will naturally, and effectively, study, pray, and give money and time to charity. Conversely, if one is dishonest in business, then prayer is insincere, study is ineffective, and charity is tainted.

How, then, can one become rich, happy, and achieve business success, while staying on the route of a higher path—an ethical, moral path? There are many religious and spiritual laws and guidelines surrounding business. In the Bible we are called to give a portion of our earnings to those who are less fortunate; we are told to pay workers promptly; to be diligent in ensuring that we charge the right amount to buyers; to help those out of work to find employment; to share information that is valuable to others; to candidly reveal any defects in our products and services; to remove obstacles from the path of other's success; to be honest and fair. According to

4

the Bible, those who act accordingly will prosper. There might be a misconception that religions spurn wealth, but in general this is not true. Religious traditions spurn ingratitude, hording, and cheating, with the recognition that gratitude, generosity, and honesty always lead to the good for all.

In Hebrew, the word for work is *avodah*, which also, surprisingly, means *prayer*. This teaches us that there is a direct connection between the physical world of work and the nonphysical world of the spirit. Both are seen as instruments of personal and social change which, when operated in harmony, reinforce each other. Just as we pray for the blessings of spiritual sustenance, we work for the blessings of physical sustenance. The connection of these words creates an understanding that work must be approached with the same reverence that we give to prayer (and, conversely, that prayer requires work, commitment, dedication, and regular practice). In this model, success at work is a blessing that eases our lives and supports and enriches those around us. This model states that, just as the world, if treated with respect, is filled with endless abundance, when work is approached with reverence there is more than enough for all. Spiritual business is based on the premise that, contrary to the common paradigm, one person's gain need not be another's loss; that success and abundance for one does not create scarcity for others.

A story is told of Safra, a poor, pious shopkeeper, who was trying to sell his donkey. One morning, as Safra was praying, a man in desperate need of a donkey approached him and offered him a price for the donkey. Because Safra was in the middle of his prayers, he could not answer. When the man saw that Safra did not respond, he assumed that his price was too low and doubled it. Again Safra did not answer, so the man tripled his price. Finally, Safra finished his prayer and said to the man,

"Your first offer was the amount that I had hoped for, and I will not use the fact that I was praying as an opportunity to get more than my asking price. I accept your first offer."

Safra received the price he needed, and the man was not exploited. A successful, ethical transaction. I like to imagine that the story continues. In my imagining, the buyer, who is clearly wealthy, recognizes in Safra a man who deals fairly. He continues to shop with Safra in the future and even directs his business associates to shop there. Soon, Safra's shop is teeming with business, the man who bought the donkey prospers, and the two men develop a friendship of trust and respect.

Safra's example sets a standard that is difficult to achieve. How many of us would have the determination to so readily turn down such an unexpected, though unearned, windfall? But this is exactly the opportunity for spiritual growth that business presents to us because when business is approached with the same spirit as prayer—with positive intention, honesty, and humility—a deeper and lasting success will naturally emerge.

I owe much of the insight on this subject to The Kabbalah of Money, *by Nilton Bonder.*

JUSTICE ON THE TRAIN

OFFERING CRITICISM

There are many places that are consciously designed to teach us spiritual lessons: churches, synagogues, mosques, ashrams, meditation centers, nature retreats, and so on. These places are usually quiet oases away from our noisy lives, where we can focus on personal growth and nurture our relationship with a higher purpose. Much of our greatest architecture is devoted to these structures, which usually rely on the powerful combination of symbolic spaces and choreographed ritual to facilitate a spiritual connection. At one time or another, the majority of Americans attend one of these places.

I'd like to suggest an addition to the list. This place does not have a grand edifice, but it shares many of the required attributes of a great spiritual center. It brings together a regular group of people in common purpose. It has ritual that is silently understood by most of its participants. For those who are so inclined, it offers the opportunity for quiet meditation, study, or meaningful dialogue with a friend, or a chance to meet someone new. On occasion, it provides a stage for high drama, where human passions are exposed and often resolved. So I'd like to suggest that we add this to our list of great spiritual places: the Metro-North New Haven commuter train.

I take this train in and out of Manhattan every weekday and have discovered that this train is a spiritual laboratory where unexpected lessons can be learned on any given day. Here, in a worn-out, narrow, long, low box, people are crowded together, forced to sit or stand close to strangers who are literally moving toward a common destination. This environment creates interactions that, normally easily avoided or dismissed, must be confronted directly. Moral, ethical, and spiritual dilemmas naturally arise, such as:

Will the standing man wake the sleeping young woman and ask that she take her bag off the adjacent seat so he can sit down? If so, will he speak to her? Will she smile at him or just grunt and go back to sleep? Should he leave her alone and accept that he must remain standing?

Will the man who is positioning himself directly in front of the opening doors move to the side to allow others to enter and leave, or will he push forward to grab one of the few remaining seats? Should someone say something? Isn't he as entitled to a seat as anyone else?

Will anyone ask the aspiring young businessman to please wait until after he has left the train to make his cell-phoned sales pitch—or at least to speak in a lower voice? Is he aware that he is disturbing others? Does he care? Should he? Who sets these rules anyway?

Should I talk to the man across the aisle who looks strangely familiar? Should I offer my seat to that elderly man standing by the door? Should I say something to the woman sitting next to me, who seems to be struggling with a painful personal issue? Can I help? Is any of this my business?

These little dramas happen daily, and I often spend my time on the train pondering these things. Recently, I witnessed an incident that dramatically illustrates an important spiritual concept. The train was docked in Grand Central Station, and I entered early—fifteen minutes before the scheduled departure time. There were very few people on the train, and I took a seat across the aisle from a young man. He had put one of his feet on the seat directly in front of him and was comfortably reading a newspaper. A middle-aged man, dressed in a crisp suit and tie, entered the train. He scanned the car and suddenly saw the man with his leg on the seat. He quickly walked over to the young man, stopped, and stood over him with his hands on his hips.

"Do you behave like this at home?" the middle-aged man asked. "Is this how you sit at home, with your feet on the furniture?"

The seated man slowly looked up from his newspaper, then quietly and sarcastically muttered, "Yes, sometimes I do," and returned to his reading.

The older man's face reddened. He pushed the young man's newspaper aside and said in a louder voice, "I'm talking to you."

"Get your hands off my paper," the other hissed. "What's your problem?"

"Get your damned foot off the seat!" the standing man shouted. "Do you think that you are the only person on this train? How is someone supposed to sit there after your filthy feet have been on it?"

"Why don't you mind your own business and go sit somewhere else?" the young man replied, his voice cracking. "There's a train full of empty seats!"

"This is my business. You are a rude, inconsiderate man, and I'll sit wherever I damn-well feel!" the middle-aged man retorted, then abruptly sat down right next to the younger man, who shook his head in disbelief.

"You gotta' be kidding me!" the young man laughed.

"We'll see who is laughing," the older man smirked. "How would you like it if I put my foot on your chair?" Then he turned and put his feet on the younger man's lap, inadvertently kicking his knee.

"You f-cking kicked me!!!" the younger man screamed. "What are you, some kinda' nut?" Then he shot up from his seat, hurried past the now-smiling older man, and muttered, "I'll just go sit elsewhere."

"Ah, another one bites the dust," the middle-aged man crowed, as he relaxed in his seat, triumphant in his victory over the forces of rudeness.

Here, on the train, was a morality drama worthy of Broadway. Actually, it was better than a Broadway play because it was real, and it carried a profound message. This was a three-minute act starring real people engaged in real struggle. The younger man had broken the rules of the train, and the older man was determined to right this heinous wrong. On the surface, it seemed to be no more than this. But the subtleties of the drama displayed an essential truth about the nature of personal criticism. Certainly the older man was right; people should not put their feet on the seats. By his actions, the offense was removed, the seat was made available for others, and the rules were enforced. Justice seemed to have been served. But was this an effective tactic? Certainly the younger man did not leave feeling that he had learned a new rule of etiquette. We can easily imagine that he will put his feet on the seat again, perhaps simply to spite the older man ("No one can tell me where to put my feet!"). We can also easily recognize that the older man did not speak to the younger man with helpful intention. He took great pleasure in his victory and seemed to have especially enjoyed shaming the younger man.

Of course, there are situations in which we should speak out; when we see that someone's actions are causing harm to himself or to others, or when we hear false statements that could lead to misunderstandings and negative outcomes. At those times we are obligated to do or say something. Unlike the older man on the train, though, how can we communicate this effectively? In The Book of Leviticus is an interesting quote about the nature of criticism that sheds some light on this question:

You will rebuke your fellow, but do not bear sin because of him.

This is an often-misunderstood quote. It requires that we correct someone who has done something wrong but then links this rebuke to bearing sin. Often this sin is seen as the failure to rebuke the wrong-doer, but this is an incorrect reading. We have to look at the words immediately preceding and following this quote to get a fuller picture. Here we find first the impassioned plea:

Do not hate your brother in your heart.

Then afterward comes the most essential statement in the entire Bible:

Love your neighbor as yourself.

The proximity of these statements teaches us that when we approach another to offer criticism, we must be sure that we do so without malice, and with the positive intent to help, as we too would like to be treated. As demonstrated by the drama on the train, an unexamined, unrestrained eagerness to criticize others can lead to unnecessary hurt, shame, and embarrassment. And in its most extreme form, we might even take pleasure in rebuking another, perhaps to satisfy an unconscious need to feel secure by dominating or controlling others, or to redress our own unexplored experience of shame. If we carry this attitude, our criticism will actually backfire, and the sin we bear as a result of our failure to treat the other with respect and compassion is our own diminished relationship with others and a weakening of our connection to the Source of our highest potential.

An unexamined, unrestrained eagerness to criticize others can lead to unnecessary hurt, shame, and embarrassment. And in its most extreme form, we might even take pleasure in rebuking another.

In his comprehensive volume about ethics, *You Shall Be Holy*, Joseph Telushkin lists six questions that we must ask ourselves before criticizing others:

1. Am I being fair, or am I exaggerating?
2. Will my words hurt the other person's feelings; and if so, how can I express myself without inflicting too much pain?
3. How would I feel if someone criticized me this way?
4. Am I enjoying the prospect of offering this criticism?
5. Is my criticism confined to a specific act or trait?
6. Are my words nonthreatening and, at least in part, reassuring?

This is a difficult and exacting list, and most of us, at times, fall short of this high standard. This may especially be a challenge when we "know" that we're right (my favorite excuse). We must be very diligent and aware, however, because when we act carelessly in criticizing, we not only hurt others, but we do, as the words of Leviticus tell us, actually damage ourselves, our spiritual growth, and our sense of well-being. When we offer criticism, we should first check our intentions and begin with a heart free of hate, followed by a commitment to compassion. Of course, you do not need to wait for a ride on the train to put this in practice....

TRY THEM, TRY THEM

DEVELOPING PERSISTENCE

Last week, I walked past a coworker's office. His door was open, and I quickly stepped in to say "hi." As I turned to leave, though, I noticed an unusual book on his credenza that immediately grabbed my attention. Most businesspeople have the typical retinue of business books in their offices—such familiar titles as *Good to Great*, *Who Moved My Cheese*, *Freakonomics*, and *The Seven Habits of Highly Effective People*. I would not have been surprised to see any of these titles in his office. This particular book caught my eye because it seemed so out of place in the office of a hard-nosed New York City real estate broker, but its orange/red cover was immediately recognizable. I knew this book intimately because I read it several times a week to my children when they were little. I smiled at him as I looked at the picture on the cover—a catlike creature standing on two feet, bent over, staring incomprehensibly at a plate of odd-looking green food. Although I hadn't opened this book in more than 15 years, I could still remember many of its familiar whimsical rhyming verses.

My coworker saw my reaction. *"Green Eggs and Ham* is the best book you'll ever read on marketing," he said with a returned smile.

Theodor Seuss Geisel, better known as Dr. Seuss, wrote *Green Eggs and Ham* in 1960, and it has been a staple of children's bedtime reading ever since. The book is a whimsical tale of two characters; one—named Sam-I-Am—is a small, energetic, enthusiastic, bright yellow creature (of some sort) with a red hat, who tries continually to convince another odd-looking creature—who is never named—to try a plate of green eggs and ham. This unnamed character is a gloomy, pale creature with a crumpled black hat, who repeatedly states that he does not like this dish, and Sam-I-Am repeatedly tries to get him to give it a taste. At the end, the unnamed creature finally consents to try the dish and, surprisingly, loves it! The two then walk off happily, arm-in-arm. That's the whole story.

On its surface, Seuss's story appears to be a simple children's story. As with all of Seuss's books (as with any enduring fable), below the charmingly quirky surface are resonant and sophisticated messages. As my coworker saw, among the messages of

Green Eggs and Ham is a lesson on one of the key elements for success in any marketing and sales strategy—persistence. Sam-I-Am refuses to give up and will not take "no" for an answer. In the end, his persistence results in a "sale" and a new loyal customer. Sam-I-Am is, in fact, an expert salesman, who uses persistence skillfully. When one approach fails, he quickly and flexibly changes tactics. As his potential client refuses to try green eggs and ham in one place, Sam-I-Am suggests that perhaps he will like them if they are tried in different locations, with different companions.

Sam-I-Am also embodies another key attribute of persistence. He faces rejection with a positive attitude. Seuss draws him as always cheerful and optimistic, even after the unnamed character flatly tells Sam-I-Am that he does not like him. How many of us could avoid taking such a remark personally and find in ourselves the determination and optimism to keep trying? In spite of this overt and caustic remark, though, Sam-I-Am happily continues to convince the other to try his product. He does so because he knows that the rejection is not personal. Sam-I-Am manages to persist cheerfully because he keeps his ego out of the picture and focuses instead on the message. Seuss's name for this character gives us a clue: Sam-I-Am. He knows exactly who he is (am?) and is comfortable with himself. He knows that the other's rejection is not a reflection of anything wrong with him as a person, but is simply an obstacle to be overcome.

There is yet another essential quality of persistence evident in Seuss's story. At the end of the

Sam-I-Am also embodies another key attribute of persistence. He faces rejection with a positive attitude.

book, after the other creature finally tries green eggs and ham, Sam-I-Am looks on proudly. He has been confident in his product all along and always believed that if the other simply tried it, he would like it. Sam-I-Am knows that green eggs and ham may sound a bit odd, and that stodgy, stubborn, complacent creatures will immediately say "no," but he also knows that green eggs and ham are delicious (though not kosher…). Sam-I-Am believes in his product and knows that what he is offering is of high quality. At the end of the book, the un-named character actually thanks Sam-I-Am for convincing him to try something new. Like Sam-I-Am, in order to sustain our enthusiasm and to ethically continue to try to convince others, it is crucial that we believe in what we are producing, saying, and selling. Blind persistence for a faulty product, service, or idea is not a virtue.

As we scratch deeper below the surface, we see that Sam-I-Am is more than a salesman. He is a spokesman for the power of persistence as a change-agent in our lives and in the lives of others. When we select a worthy goal and persist in our commitment to see it through, regardless of rejection and self-doubt, we can overcome almost any obstacle and limitation. As we know, this is not easy. Along the way, setbacks may tempt us to lose confidence. Naysayers may convince us that we cannot achieve our vision. We may simply decide that we are too tired to continue. Dr. Seuss lightly and humorously tells us that the force of optimism will always overcome that of pessimism, if we can only consistently muster the determination to keep going.

Sam-I-Am is more than a salesman. He is a spokesman for the power of persistence as a change-agent in our lives and in the lives of others.

So what lessons have we learned so far about the quality of persistence from Dr. Seuss?

- Don't give up.
- When one approach fails, try something new.
- Stay optimistic.
- Don't take rejection personally.
- Believe in what you are pursuing.

Dr. Seuss also teaches a more subtle, spiritual lesson on the nature of persistence. At the beginning of the book, we find the un-named creature sitting comfortably in an armchair, reading a newspaper. Sam-I-Am bursts in on a fantastical vehicle, carrying a plate of the unusual dish, announcing change, risk, and the possibility of something new, shattering the other's comfort zone. The un-named creature resists, stating that he does not like this change, even though he has never even tried it. In this way, Dr. Seuss's creatures are archetypes for the struggle between our inclination to settle for the status quo and our ambitions to create change; between our craving for energy and our attraction to lethargy; between a desire to try something adventurous and the lure of playing it safe. The un-named creature, sitting safely in his chair, is called to try something new; something that he may actually like; something that will change the way he views the world. Yet he continually resists. His resistance, however, is not based on facts or experience, but is a stubborn refusal to respond to this call—a refusal to enter the unknown and accept the risk that comes with changing his old habits.

In the end, the un-named creature finds himself in the dark, on a runaway train, plummeting into the ocean, submerged in open waters, surrounded by strange onlookers, as Sam-I-Am asks yet again, "Try it?" At the end of his rope, his resistance worn out, this stubborn creature finally agrees and, to his surprise and delight, instantly finds that the thing he has been so actively resisting—the thing that has taken him completely out of his comfort zone—is actually good for him. Sam-I-Am is his persistent messenger for change, who will not let him off the hook and who continually reappears until the change is embraced.

At its deepest level, Dr. Seuss's book is a story about the persistence of the call to growth and change. If you have experienced this phenomenon, you know that, somehow, the same message continues to reappear in your life—perhaps in different guises, from different people and different situations—and that this message will continue to pursue you until you consent to listen and act. Then, like the un-named creature, you suddenly discover that the thing you have been resisting is actually good, and you are then grateful that the unwelcome messenger, consistent in his message, had the persistence to not give up on you. This persistence softened you, wore down your natural resistance, and made you receptive to change. As a saying from an anonymous author teaches:

> *In the confrontation between the stream and the rock, the stream always wins. Not through strength, but through persistence.*

Now, perhaps you may think that this is an overly ambitious reading of a simple children's book. Well, maybe so. But try it, try it!

DOOR OPENERS

SPIRITUAL LEADERSHIP

Nearly a decade ago, I was scanning the business section of a local bookstore, hoping to find a book that would help me be more effective in a new leadership position at my job. A particular title caught my eye: *The Tao of Leadership: Lao Tzu's Tao Te Ching Adapted for a New Age*, written in 1985 by John Heider. The inside book jacket noted:

> *The Tao of Leadership is an invaluable tool for anyone in a position of leadership. This book provides the most simple and clear advice on how to be the very best kind of leader: be faithful, trust the process, pay attention, and inspire others to become their own leaders.*

Here was a book that took the teaching from the *Tao Te Ching*, the 2,500-year-old philosophical text that is central to Chinese religions, as a guide for modern business leadership. I smiled as I put the book back on the shelf, thinking that this was just a clever gimmick. I soon noticed another eye-catching title, though: *Jesus, CEO: Using Ancient Wisdom for Visionary Leadership*, by Laurie Beth Jones. I quickly checked to make sure that I had not accidentally walked into the Religion section of the bookstore (my usual stomping ground). Clearly, there was a trend at work here—melding spiritual practice with business leadership. Since then, this trend seems to have accelerated. If you search Google for book titles with the keyword *leadership*, you will find among the thousands of results such titles as *Spiritual Leadership*, *Spiritual Discipleship*, *Courageous Leadership*, *Spirituality and Ethics at Work*, *The Cost of Moral Leadership*, and *The Good Book on Leadership*. Now, in fact, it is getting difficult to tell where the Spirituality/Religion section ends and the Business section begins.

What's going on here? It appears that leading thinkers and teachers in the field of business management are looking toward spiritual and religious traditions as a source for guiding modern business leaders. For those of us who have been in the workplace for many years, this is an unexpected trend. The traditional model of leadership that many of us have learned and experienced seems very distant from the arena of spirituality. In the past, leaders were often either born into the position through the benefits of high class and lineage or rose through the ranks based on self-publicized accomplishments, personal ambition, impressing the boss, and out-maneuvering the competition. Often, however, these leaders were blatantly amoral, following the Machiavellian belief that the ends justify the means, and their subordinates simply accepted that this kind of tough-minded management style was part of a leader's necessary make-up. In the past, leaders often surrounded themselves with religious figures, relying on the power of organized religion to both support and justify their position. But these leaders were typically not expected to embody spiritual ideals themselves.

Now, the model has dramatically changed, and a successful modern business leader is held to a higher moral and ethical standard. Perhaps this is due to the increasing mobility of our culture, a higher-educated workforce, generally strong economy, and the culture change initiated by the Baby Boomers' questioning of authority. Or maybe it's a result of the new requirements of business ethics regulations, greater transparency created by communication technology, or even of a general societal spiritual awakening. Whatever the case, the effect is

The traditional model of leadership that many of us have learned and experienced seems very distant from the arena of spirituality.

that employees simply will not be motivated to produce their best work and will not stay in a job where the boss is abusive, dishonest, or self-centered—hence, the influx of books and seminars designed to teach leaders new skills based on spiritual, religious, and ethical qualities.

To be effective, the new business leaders must embody this new model of leadership. We all recognize such leaders when we meet them. There is something about these people that draws us to them, encouraging us to perform at our highest level and to work together toward a worthwhile goal, while providing us with the security that the right person is at the helm. This is a genuine connection of trust that is not based on power, coercion, title, or position. The new business leader, though, cannot simply mimic prescribed "spiritual" qualities—such as caring and listening—because mimics are soon revealed by their inconsistencies and are eventually distrusted (the classic caricature of this is Bill Lumbergh, the smirking, phony, self-involved boss from the movie *Office Space*). These new leadership qualities need to be internalized rather than imitated. This is a practice that begins as an inward

The new business leader, though, cannot simply mimic prescribed "spiritual" qualities—such as caring and listening.

28

journey, with the conscious intent of personal growth. In essence, then, business leadership is a spiritual practice.

Whatever strategies, tactics, or techniques of leadership may be presented in training sessions and books, the essential requirement for an effective leader is the genuine commitment to his/her own spiritual development. The more seriously one delves into business leadership , the more one finds it to be spiritual practice. In his book, *Leadership in Organizations*, Gary Yukl noted:

> *It is difficult to become a sensitive, caring, and empowering leader unless you have reached a high level of emotional and moral development.*

What all these books that blend spirituality and business leadership tell us is that the qualities that nurture the spirit are exactly the same qualities that make an effective leader. These qualities include the following:

- A passionate, selfless vision based on an alignment with a higher purpose, outside of ego-driven desires.
- The discipline and commitment to implement a meaningful vision, relying on a diverse team of motivated individuals.
- Empathy and compassion for others, resulting in the desire to inspire them to rise to their highest potential.

- The humility to listen to others with respect, and to sincerely consider their opinions.
- The ability to balance conviction with flexibility and intellect with intuition.
- The commitment to speak and act truthfully.
- The courage to re-examine personal beliefs and to change them when faced with new facts.
- An unshakable optimism, rooted in the knowledge that people, and the world, are inherently good.

Here, then, is a bold statement:

The most effective leaders (in any field) are those who are most spiritually evolved.

The great leaders who have created positive sustained change are all highly evolved spiritual beings. Abraham Lincoln, for example, surrounded himself with those who vehemently opposed his position. He did this in order to continually evaluate his beliefs by testing them against the harshest criticism. He had the courage to look at himself honestly and to respectfully listen to and consider divergent opinions. Lincoln agonized over decisions that would put young soldiers in harm's way and was racked with grief over the enormous loss of life. Yet he knew that the future of his beloved country required victory.

In current times, CEOs like Jeffrey Swartz of Timberland Shoes have demonstrated the power of living their values and of embodying spiritual principles. Timberland has been a leader in implementing energy-reducing technology and other ways to reduce their carbon emissions, well before this became a national concern and visible trend. Swartz even pays employees to volunteer in the community. His balance sheet reports the "double bottom line"—gains in profit and values.

Spiritual leadership is not a learned skill or practiced technique. Ultimately, there is no proven recipe. In their book, *The Leadership Challenge*, Kouzes and Posner examined a wide array of effective leaders, and conclude:

> *We've said that leaders take us to places we've never been before. But there are no freeways to the future, no paved highways to unknown, unexplored destinations. There's only wilderness. To step out into the unknown, begin with the exploration of the inner territory. With that as a base, we can then discover and unleash the leader within us all.*

By embracing a commitment to the highest spiritual and moral standards, effective leaders present an example for all to emulate. Mahatma Gandhi, who showed the world that peaceful, determined, and spiritual dedication to a just cause can create radical change, taught the essential truth about leadership:

> *I must first be the change I want to see in my world.*

Ultimately, effective leaders simply help point us in a new direction, open a door of new possibilities, and encourage us to enter, stop for a moment, and look around.

WHO NEEDS YOU?

WORKING TOGETHER

A 2003 national survey revealed an interesting and surprising result. A representative sampling of Americans was asked this question: "What do you think is the most important factor in getting ahead in the workplace?" Ranked ahead of the expected answers such as "merit and performance," "leadership skills," "intelligence," "making money for the organization," and "working long hours," was the top answer—"being a team player."

Perhaps this was not so surprising after all. Almost anyone in the workplace today has heard of the importance of teamwork in business, and a myriad of books and seminars have touted the value of working in a team (perhaps you even work in a "team configuration" environment). Do we really know what "teamwork" is, though? An entire branch of management theory has emerged around the concept of teaming and has developed specific criteria and qualities that are needed to make a successful team. Teamwork, we learn, is much more than merely being part of a larger group. In 1993, British researcher Meredith Belbin proposed nine roles that successful teams should have:

The Coordinator: This person has the skills and temperament needed to bring the team together and facilitate consensus. Such an individual is typically mature and calm and is a skilled communicator and listener.

The Shaper: This person helps bring the team's decisions to quantifiable and achievable goals by assimilating various viewpoints in to a clear vision. This role requires an optimistic outlook, diplomatic temperament, and flexible attitude.

The Plant: This person challenges the team to look beyond standard answers through a creative approach and unconventional thinking. Such an individual is typically artistic and passionate and is bored by, and suspicious of, ready, tried solutions.

The Resource Investigator: This person has deep contacts and knows how to leverage connections to bring relevant information and individuals to the team. This role requires someone who is outgoing and friendly and who can build strong relationships.

The Implementer: This person is very organized, thinks linearly, and is effective at turning big ideas into manageable tasks. A good implementer is methodical, logical, and hardworking, and most highly values precision, quality, and commitment.

The Team Worker: The Team Worker is concerned with the individual needs of the team and works to mediate conflict and promote harmony. This person is caring and empathetic, and enjoys supporting the efforts of others.

The Completer: As the title suggests, the Completer is the one who drives the deadlines and makes sure they are achieved. This person is conscientious and process-driven, and focuses on meeting the agreed-upon team goals.

The Monitor Evaluator: This person quickly reacts to change and develops new strategies and solutions as needed. The Monitor Evaluator is most concerned with moving the team forward by pushing through adversity and effectively solving problems.

The Specialist: This is an individual who possesses specific information needed by the team to perform the task. The Specialist may tend to be narrowly focused and will typically not see the entire picture. Specialists admire education and depth of knowledge.

Of course, not every team needs these nine specific members, and many of these roles are often carried by one person. But as this list tells us, no one single person can be all these roles, because an effective team requires a diverse range of personalities—

from those who are detail-oriented, to those who are big-picture focused; from extroverted and creative, to conservative and reserved. Perhaps you recognize yourself or your coworkers in some of these roles. Perhaps you relate well to one role, or perhaps you flinch when you read another. This list points out that we need diversity to create an effective team and that a wide variety of people is needed.

> *An effective team requires a diverse range of personalities—from those who are detail-oriented, to those who are big-picture focused; from extroverted and creative, to conservative and reserved.*

What is most striking about this list is the realization that the qualities that we may find challenging, disagreeable, or —let's be honest—even annoying in others, are just the qualities that are needed to round out the team. So instead of complaining about the person whose characteristics are different than your own, you can:

- Thank goodness for the *detail-maniac* who drives you crazy with endless picky questions. This person makes sure that your team produces an accurate, quality product.

- Thank goodness for the *irresponsible flake* who interferes with the linearity of the process. This person brings fresh ideas to your sometimes-stale thinking.
- Thank goodness for the *control-freak* who insists that everything occurs exactly as planned. This person ensures that the schedule is met.
- Thank goodness for the smiling *glad-hander* who seems to always be out schmoozing instead of working. This person brings new resources and support to your team.
- Thank goodness for the *glowering critic* who constantly finds fault in everything that is produced. This person picks up the pieces when the inevitable change of plan occurs.
- And thank goodness for *you*, who is probably one of these annoying folks to somebody else.

By participating in conscious teamwork, we surround ourselves with others who possess different skills and temperaments. We need diversity because none of us is complete enough to provide all that is required. So the person whose qualities most conflict with yours is probably the person you most need on your team. Imagine a team filled with people exactly like you! Everyone with exactly the same skill sets, the same outlook, the same attitudes, the same beliefs…. If you've ever seen the eccentric movie *Being John Malkovich*, you may remember the scene when the actor travels into his own "brain portal" and experiences a reality in which everyone looks and acts exactly like himself. He emerges screaming from this, his worst possible nightmare.

The person whose qualities most conflict with yours is probably the person you most need on your team.

By being engaged in a diverse team, we learn life skills that we would not develop in a monolithic group nor on our own. Foremost, we develop the skill of listening. When there are others with different opinions and points of view, we can either shut them out or open ourselves to their ideas. Through this process, we increase our capacity for empathy and compassion. We also learn the gentle art of persuasion. In a like-minded group, no one needs to be persuaded. In a diverse team, though, individuals are encouraged to exchange, defend, and possibly rethink their ideas. Finally, and most importantly, a diverse team develops respect. We learn to respect the views of others, and perhaps to respectably agree to disagree.

What teamwork ultimately teaches is to embrace the value of diversity, especially when the other person's role is most different from yours. There is a wonderful Buddhist teaching that encourages us to seek out those who are most different from ourselves—who most challenge our beliefs—and to engage them as our teachers. This tradition realizes that such a person can open our hearts and minds to new ways of thinking that had been hidden from us and that we would never have discovered alone. The person who most "pushes our buttons," then, can be our greatest asset. This can be a tremendously hard lesson to learn, but one that, if lived, can have the potential for profound growth and powerful transformation.

We see that the world is filled with endless diversity, all created with a very specific purpose. And thank goodness for that. After all, we are ultimately all part of a very, very large team, and the respect for each other's unique roles is crucial to our collective future.

Listen Up

Effective Listening

In the previous chapter, "Who Needs You?," we discussed the value and power of teamwork—that by working in a team, we promote diversity, and that embracing those with different temperaments and inclinations ensures that all aspects of a project are addressed. As noted, to effectively communicate within a diverse team, we must develop three essential skills:

1. Respect
2. Persuasion
3. Listening

These are all core skills, and each one is worthy of separate in-depth study. The respect we show others is a key to building meaningful relationships. And the ability to persuasively present our own point of view is essential for success. What about listening, though? At first, listening hardly even seems to fit in the category of "skill" and appears to be primarily a passive sensory activity with little demonstration of any specific skill sets.

Over the last half-century, though, mainstream management theory has promoted the concept of listening as a skill that can increase sales and improve communication. Now there are many books and seminars that teach us how to be better listeners. Many of these teach actionable skills such as the following:

- Lean forward and make eye contact when others speak in order to show that you are engaged in the conversation.
- Nod or tilt your head in order to demonstrate that you have heard what was said.
- Repeat back what the other person has said to signal that you have understood.

I have been to seminars that teach these listening skills (at the encouragement of the victims of my often absent-minded listening) and have tried to use these skills in my personal and business lives. I've discovered that making eye contact, leaning in to the conversation, nodding, repeating, and other external demonstrations, are all good tips if you want to present a convincing image of an engaged listener. But somehow, I must admit, these *skills* haven't really helped much, and every year I rewrite the same New Year's resolution: "Become a better listener!"

And every year I ask the same questions: "How can I actually become a better listener?" and "What's the real value of listening?"

Let's first look at these questions from the perspective of business. In their best-seller, *The One Minute Salesperson*, Larry Wilson and Spencer Johnson write:

> *The best salespeople are good listeners—that's how you find out what the buyer wants.*

This is a clear and obvious observation. If we want to sell a product or service to a customer, we need to first hear what it is that the customer needs so we can devise a solution. But how often have we misunderstood what the customer has told us, delivered the wrong product or service, or missed additional opportunities because we didn't really understand what the customer was telling us? Maybe we only gleaned the surface of the conversation. Perhaps we were busier trying to convince our customers to hire us than listening to their needs. Poor listening can be costly, leading to mistakes, bad service, misaligned goals, wasted time, and lack of teamwork. If we had *really* listened, perhaps we might have discovered a way to more fully meet our clients' needs, and we would have been more successful. President Calvin Coolidge remarked with his famous brevity:

> *No man ever listened himself out of a job.*

Listening is very complex , though. Studies have shown that up to 93% of communication is non-verbal, including tone of voice, eye movement, posture, hand gestures, facial expressions, and others. As we know, even a simple statement like, "That's great," can carry a multitude of messages. Said with the wide eyes of enthusiasm, or the frown of jealousy, or the down-turned glance of resignation, or the smile of approval, or the snicker of sarcasm, "That's great," can mean almost anything. Truly understanding the speaker's intention, then, requires an immersion in the complete message sent by the speaker, far beyond the mere words used.

As Steven Covey notes in *The Seven Habits of Highly Effective People*, one of the vital characteristics of an effective person is:

First seek to understand, then to be understood.

Covey is saying that we must put ourselves and our agenda to the side so that we can completely concentrate on what the other person is saying. You cannot concentrate on the other person when you are focused on your own image, formulating your response, or pushing your agenda. Good listening, then, begins with the determination to focus your attention outward, toward the other, and away from yourself. Then, as Steven Covey notes, only after you have fully understood the other person's message should you begin to explain yours. This is the true skill of listening and when routinely practiced

will produce profound sensitivity and awareness.

In spiritual and reli-
gious jargon, this need to
put our own needs to
the side is often called
"negation of the ego" and
is the first step in any spiri-

*Only after you have
fully understood the
other person's mes-
sage should you
begin to explain
yours.*

tual practice. For those of you who have ever meditated, you may have learned that the meditative
practice begins by concentrating on the simple act of
breathing, or on watching the flicker of a candle, or
staring at a geometric image, or repeating a simple
phrase. The idea here is to place your attention on
something that will take you away from yourself—
from the chatter of your own mind, the agitation of
your own emotions, and even the sensations of your
own body—in order to let something more subtle
and profound enter your awareness. This teaching—
that listening is an essential skill for personal growth
and success—can also be found in many places in
the Bible. The central and most ancient Jewish
prayer, the *Sh'ma*, which comes from The Book of
Deuteronomy, begins with the powerful imperative:
"Listen!" This prayer makes it clear that the first step
in spiritual growth is the commitment to truly and
deeply listen.

From another episode in the Bible comes a
phrase about listening that has entered the common
language. In this story, the prophet Elijah is found

high in the mountains, hiding from a corrupt leadership that wants to silence his message of reform. He cries out to the heavens in despair, asking to understand his suffering. Suddenly there is a great wind, then an earthquake, then fire. But he does not find his answer in any of these. Then, unexpectedly, he hears a "still small voice," and is comforted. It was only when Elijah put aside all personal distractions (wind, earthquake, and fire can be seen as metaphors for the constant inner noises that distract us from being receptive to others and to the Divine) that he could truly listen and understand. As this story teaches, listening is a subtle, quiet activity, which is directed away from ourselves and our own egos. When we are focused on our own needs, are distracted, or are impatient with the conversation, we stop listening. Deep listening requires the courage to put ourselves and our needs aside for a moment, to let the conversation evolve toward an understanding of the other, and to truly hear in the still small voice the real message.

Two final quotes about the power of listening: First, the business writer Peter Nulty, notes:

> *Of all the skills of leadership, listening is the most valuable—and least understood. Most captains of industry listen only sometimes, and they remain ordinary leaders. But a few, the great ones, never stop listening. That's how they get word before anyone else of unseen problems and opportunities.*

And finally, my favorite quote about listening, which lightly and succinctly sums it up, comes from the flamboyant playwright and entrepreneur, Wilson Mizner:

A good listener is not only popular everywhere, but after a while he knows something.

I Don't Know

Respectful Conversation

In almost every home in America, especially in homes with young children, there is a special place. This place serves many purposes. It is the repository for much that is immediately important. It displays the great recent achievements of the family, directs activities, and often holds words of wisdom or encouragement. Temporarily adhered to its metal surface are the children's latest masterpieces and report cards, schedules of important upcoming events, or pictures of beloved family and friends. Of course I'm talking about the domestic holy of holies—the kitchen refrigerator door. And because we cannot avoid looking at it every time we reach for a snack or cold drink, many people place inspirational messages on this door. For many years, I had such a printed message, which occupied a special place of honor right next to the ice dispenser. It read:

Seven qualities characterize the fool and the wise man:

1. *The wise man does not speak before someone wiser than him.*
2. *He does not break in to his fellow's speech.*
3. *He is not in a rush to reply.*
4. *He asks what is relevant and replies to the point.*
5. *He speaks of first things first and last things last.*
6. *Of what he has not heard he says, "I have not heard."*
7. *And he acknowledges what is true.*

The opposites apply to the fool.

This saying comes from *Pirkei Avot (The Sayings of the Fathers),* a collection of short aphorisms from The Talmud—the compilation of Jewish Bible interpretation—that address ethical action. Although this saying is nearly two thousand years old, it spoke directly to an issue that I and, I believe, many of us, struggle with almost daily: how to respectfully engage others in meaningful conversation. I read this every morning as I reached for the milk and every evening after returning from work. When I moved to New York several years ago, however, the paper on which this saying was printed disappeared. I still keep these seven qualities listed in my mind, though, and they continue to yield insights and challenges well beyond their apparently simple message.

An issue that I and, I believe, many of us, struggle with almost daily: how to respectfully engage others in meaningful conversation.

On its surface, this saying from *Pirkei Avot* addresses issues of proper, polite speech and provides guidelines for respectful dialogue. These are essential points, and when taken to heart will help us to engage others more effectively. This saying tells us to listen to what others have to say, to not interrupt, to stay on topic, to not make up answers to that which we do not know, and to recognize the truth, even if it's different from our cherished opinions or points of view. How often have we been in a meeting, presentation, or casual conversation, and experienced someone who constantly interrupts, or who impatiently waits for others to finish so he can jump in with his opinion? Or will change the subject or fabricate an answer? Or will not consider that he might be wrong, and that someone else might be right? We can experience this person as a take-charge type or perhaps as an arrogant know-it-all, or maybe as one who is just plain rude. And let's be honest, how often have we been that person? (This was on *my* refrigerator, after all.)

It's all too easy to fall into these patterns because it's all too easy to believe that there is a good reason to do so. When we are engaged in conversation, especially when we are trying to come across well—to a client, a new acquaintance, our boss, our spouse—it seems natural to want to put forward a strong opinion to impress; to show we know what we're talking about (I'm informed!), to direct the conversation (I'm a leader!), to demonstrate our value (I'm important!), to move attention toward us (I'm confident!), to entertain (I'm clever!), or to avoid appearing shy, aloof, or disinterested, (well, at least I'm sociable!). We might have been taught that we should never appear "weak" in front of others and that, therefore, we should not admit we don't know something. We might then believe we should redirect the subject when faced with a topic for which we have no knowledge, or we should not back down from our expressed opinion, or allow another to be right. We may think that if we are quiet and yield to others, or candidly acknowledge that we simply don't know, we'll be seen as ineffective or unnecessary.

What's extraordinary about the saying from *Pirkei Avot* is that it turns this conventional wisdom on its head. We usually believe that the person who answers quickly, interrupts, and always knows the answer must be very secure and competent. We tend to associate verbal assertiveness, quick wit, and ready answers with the wise person—with one who is confident. We also tend to associate one who is silent, deferential, and readily says, "I don't know," with the fool—with one who is insecure and incompetent. This saying from *Pirkei Avot* teaches just the opposite. This saying teaches us that wisdom comes from the basic humility of accepting that we do not know everything, that others know things that we do not, and that life involves continual learning.

Wisdom comes from the basic humility of accepting that we do not know everything, that others know things that we do not, and that life involves continual learning.

When we do not adhere to these principles; when we refuse to recognize that there are others who may know more than we and who have valuable information to share, then, according to *Pirkei Avot*, we are acting foolish. When we don't take the time to listen to others, or we think our opinion is the most important, or we can't allow ourselves to simply say, "I don't know," we have become foolish because we shut ourselves off from new learning. We do this, ultimately, out of insecurity, not confidence. Insecurity stems from a lack of confidence in our own essential goodness and worth. This sense that "there is something wrong with me," if not examined and healed, creates a false defensive front that is built on the belief that I should not expose those parts of myself that feel like flaws because I will then be found wanting and will be rejected. And, because I don't approve of myself as I am, I then seek external approval of my false front to reassure me that I am, in fact, good enough. But the image I am presenting is not really me, so therefore my natural ability to honestly and deeply connect with others is dulled. What began as insecurity and need for approval finally takes the external form of arrogance, insensitivity, or lack of humility. This produces the opposite results from the initial—usually unconscious—intention, which is to receive approval. Due to my appearance of arrogance I now get less approval, and consequently my belief there is something wrong with me is reinforced, creating more insecurity. So the false front thickens to further protect me, leading to even less approval. As a result of this process, growth is slowed or stopped because when I cannot simply allow myself to admit the "weakness" of not knowing, I cannot successfully learn.

The saying from *Pirkei Avot* offers a way out of the painful and destructive cycle by telling us that wisdom springs from the realization that we don't need to protect ourselves from exposure or prove ourselves worthy and that we can respectfully open ourselves to receive what others have to say. Once we become comfortable with this basic truth, we readily accept that there is always someone who has knowledge we lack. We do not interrupt this person because we appreciate the other's valuable knowledge. We do not rush to answer because we want to be sure that the other is finished speaking. We weigh our answer carefully because we desire to understand and be understood. We do not change the subject because we are comfortable with the realization that there is an infinite amount of possible knowledge. And when asked something we do not know, we readily admit this because we see the opportunity to learn something new. This is true wisdom, according to the saying from *Pirkei Avot*, and it arises from the deep security that births genuine humility.

From the Tao Te Ching, the Chinese "Book of the Way," comes this essential realization:

> *Those who try to outshine others dim their own light...Those who boast of their own accomplishments diminish the things they've done.*

This dynamic is a central understanding of all religious and spiritual teachings. The greatest teachers, including Moses, Buddha, and Jesus, are all noted for their profound wisdom coupled with deep humility and deference to others.

Twenty years ago, when I was new to the business world, I was, like many young people, so eager to prove myself that I often resisted admitting what

I did not know and was reluctant to ask for help out of fear that I'd appear incompetent. Fortunately, I had a boss who saw right through this fragile façade. One day, as we were discussing a project (and I was, as usual, trying to make a good impression), he suddenly looked right at me, and with a small smile, said,

"Alan, you know, I have a little practice that I've developed over the years that is very helpful. At least once a day, I try to say 'I don't know,' and to do or say something that makes me appear a little awkward, or even foolish. Usually, though," he added through a light chuckle, "I don't even have to try."

At the time, I could not understand his strange comment. How could this person—a successful, respected businessman—advocate appearing unknowledgeable and, heaven forbid, foolish? Now, I am beginning to understand his sensitive and timely advice, and my regular spiritual practice includes the commitment to appreciate the opportunity to ask for help and to admit that which I don't know.

John Godfrey Saxe, a nineteenth-century American poet, wrote a well-known poem titled, "The Essence of an Elephant." This poem tells of six blind men from Indostan who attempt to understand an elephant. The first blind man touches the side of the elephant and determines that an elephant is, in essence, a wall. The second touches the tusk and determines that an elephant is a spear. The third touches the trunk and determines that an elephant is a snake; then the others touch the ear, leg, and tail, all with different proclamations on the nature of the elephant. The poem ends with the six blind men arguing about which is right:

> *And so these men of Indostan disputed loud and long,*
>
> *Each in his own opinion, exceeding stiff and strong,*
>
> *Though each was partly in the right, all were in the wrong!*

Each thought he knew all that was knowable about the elephant and stubbornly defended his own position, refusing to learn from the others, yet each only grasped a small piece of the whole. Their insistence that each knew best kept them all in the dark. These are the type of fools that *Pirkei Avot* warns against.

So the next time you are tempted to interrupt, jump in with a quick comment, or are reluctant to admit that you don't know something, take a mental walk to the refrigerator door, and ask yourself, who is wise, and who is foolish?

IN THE BEGINNING

KEEPING RESOLUTIONS

(This message was delivered for the New Year, 2008, and continues the theme introduced in "I Don't Know").

Happy New Year! I wish you and your families a year of health, happiness, and prosperity. The observance of the New Year is possibly the oldest of all holidays. We have records of New Year celebrations dating back to ancient Mesopotamia, nearly 4,000 years ago. These records indicate that people then participated in one of today's most popular and potent aspects of this holiday: the making of New Year's resolutions. Most of us still make resolutions for the New Year, promising, perhaps, to spend more time with family and friends, lose weight, get fit, make more money, get organized, learn something new, help others…. For us, as for our ancestors, the New Year offers an opportunity to start again, with the determination that tomorrow will be better than yesterday.

Humanity seems to have a need for the possibility of a fresh start. Most religions recognize that cyclical events, such as the New Year, bring the promise of personal growth and a better world. Judaism, Christianity, and Islam, for example, commemorate the end of each week with a Sabbath—a day of rest and contemplation, when we can put the previous week behind us and start again. We need this chance to begin again. Beginnings are crucial to our growth. As Plato, the founder of Western philosophy, taught:

> *The beginning is the most important part of the work.*

Beginnings, though, often fizzle out, and the fresh start that we dreamed of, planned, and planted, just does not seem to bloom. Most people begin their New Year's resolutions with great enthusiasm and commitment, but, as we've all experienced, these resolutions can quickly dissolve as we soon return to our comfortable, predictable patterns. There are many reasons for this phenomenon. Perhaps we discover that we simply don't have the time to implement the change. Or we find that the results we desired did not come as quickly as we had expected. Or we simply lose steam and give up. We know, however, that these reasons are usually just excuses for avoiding the new start that we had hoped for.

The Book of Proverbs offers an insight and guidance on how we can overcome these obstacles and

Humanity seems to have the need for the possibility of a fresh start.

60

begin in a way that is sustainable. A sentence from Proverbs 9:10—often misunderstood because English does not capture the deeper meaning of its message, and the subtlety of its words—tells us that:

Wisdom begins with the humble awareness of the Infinite.

This Proverb teaches that beginnings require wisdom and that wisdom begins with the existential knowledge that you are guided and supported in your life, and with the simple recognition of the most obvious, most unavoidable truth: You, unlike God, are finite, changeable, and fallible. To begin with wisdom, then, means to admit that, as a human being, you are meant to grow. And growth comes when you expose yourself to missteps, mistakes, wrong turns, and even to risk failure, knowing that this journey will lead you where you are meant to go— or at least with the sense that you might learn something along the way. In another well-known Talmudic aphorism, Rabbi Ben Zoma asks, "Who is wise?" and answers, "One who learns from everyone [and everything]. From all those who taught me I gained understanding." Ben Zoma encourages us to put aside our limiting assumptions of where we can learn and who can teach us, and, most importantly, the defenses of our egos ("I have nothing to learn from you!"), in order for new knowledge and experiences to emerge. After all, who knows what you may learn from unexpected sources? In the face of

the vast amount of possible knowledge and understanding, we are always students and beginners. As
Thomas Edison famously remarked:

*We don't even begin to understand one percent
about ninety percent of anything.*

The Buddhists have a very sophisticated practice
for embracing this way of thinking. Called, appropriately, "Beginner's Mind," this practice helps us to
start again. In his book, *Zen Mind Beginner's Mind*,
the Zen priest, Shunryu Suzuki, wrote:

*If your mind is empty, it is always ready for
everything. It is open to everything. In the
beginners mind there are many possibilities; in
the expert's mind there are few. In the beginners
mind there is no thought "I have attained something." All self-centered thoughts limit our vast
mind. When we have no thought of self, no
thought of achievement, we are true beginners.*

Beginner's Mind teaches us to abandon our self-
defeating beliefs: our impulse to think, "That's not
how it works," "That can't be done," "That won't
work," or "Who are you to teach me?" and instead
embraces the thoughts, "Wow, I didn't know that!,"
"That's fascinating," and "Please tell me more!" In this
way, we always remain beginners, no matter how
much we have learned or experienced. This doesn't
mean, of course, that we should shun the pursuit
of expertise or that we should not be proud of
our knowledge and accomplishments. Skills and
knowledge are required if we are to accomplish

anything meaningful and be of assistance to others. Beginner's Mind, though, encourages us to always approach life as learners. This attitude creates the possibility of new starts and the ability to implement our new resolutions with openness, flexibility, enthusiasm, and joy.

There is a well-known Zen saying, popularized by the singer Donovan in the 1960s, which summarizes this growth process toward wisdom:

First there is a mountain, then there is not a mountain, then there is.

This saying poetically describes the development of Beginner's Mind through the simple example of a mountain. First, in our youth, we see mountains with the unrestrained wonder of a child: giant, mysterious, unknowable objects that reach to the clouds. To a child, that's a mountain. Then we learn about mountains—how they are created by tectonic movement in the earth's crust, pushed up gradually over eons, made up of layers of rock formed by the planet's molten interior, and hardened in the atmosphere. We give the mountains names, measure their height, and determine their age. Now we think that we understand mountains and soon move on to the next topic. The essence of the mountain, though, is now lost. The mountain ceases to exist ("then there is no mountain") once we say that because we think we have learned all there is to learn, we know it, understand it, and have finished our exploration.

63

Later, with maturity, humility, and wisdom, we discover that the labels and measurements are good factual information, but don't do anything to help us truly know the mountain. We rediscover that the mountain is much more than we can understand. We can see again the incredible mystery of the mountain, appreciate its beauty, feel its power, discover that it is a component in a delicate ecosystem shaped by its very presence, and even begin to see the movements of the earth's crust that created it as part of a larger plan, in an infinitely complex, purposeful system in which we, like the mountain, are participants. Again, the mountain re-appears, but now in a mature way that is *child-like* in its potential, but not *childish*. The knowledge that we gained earlier, when we thought that we were "experts" about the mountain, is now integrated into a new, larger, more subtle wisdom. Because the mountain has infinite possibilities, no one can claim to be a complete "expert" on it, and new learning is always available. We now have a humble awareness of the Infinite.

With the New Year, when we resolve to begin anew—to implement the changes that we know we need—we can remember that, in fact, the possibility to start over is available at any and every moment, once we accept this challenge with the attitude of a beginner.

PRELUDE TO DISASTER

BUILDING CONFIDENCE

In most of these messages, I like to include relevant quotes in order to illuminate, support, and clarify the subject being discussed. These quotes come from religious scriptures, philosophers, statesmen, business leaders, and poets, and these sources demonstrate the fact that basic truths cross easily over physical, temporal, religious, and cultural boundaries. As we enter the upcoming fall season at work, and we are all gearing up to redouble our efforts, a particular well-known quote has been coming to my mind:

He who hesitates is lost.

These words were written by Alexander Pope, the great eighteenth-century English poet. Most of us know these words, and perhaps we may think that we understand its message: Don't delay when opportunity knocks on your door. This is only half the quote, though. The remainder of Pope's words provides a much clearer understanding of his intent:

Swift and resolute action leads to success; self-doubt is a prelude to disaster.

The full quote tells us that we must overcome self-doubt so that we can act confidently, with speed and resolve. We all immediately recognize this as true. For most of us, though, overcoming self-doubt is a difficult, life-long struggle. The average person, I've read, processes over 60,000 thoughts per day, of which 90% occur subconsciously. Although many of these thoughts are positive, many of them are inevitably negative, and the majority of those negative thoughts are not conscious, but pop up unbidden, possibly out of developed habit or inclination. I've discovered that my negative thoughts, for example, are usually based on exaggerations or distortions of events that happened in the past that I've classified as disappointments or failures. This then produces worries about my current and future challenges, leading to self-doubt. As Pope dramatically notes, such self-doubt undermines the ability to act successfully. This is because our thoughts can produce self-fulfilling consequences. Negative thoughts, words, and attitudes lead to negative and unhappy moods and actions, creating negative results, and more self-doubt. Conversely, positive thinking, when practiced regularly, promotes decisive action and increased energy, which leads to success and confidence. As Henry Ford advised:

Whether you think you can or think you can't—you are right.

What can we do when the inevitable, usually subconscious, negative thoughts arise, though? How can we, as Pope recommends, put aside self-doubt, especially when it seems to arise automatically? Another quote provides some guidance:

Don't be content with things as they are. 'The earth is yours and the fullness thereof.' Enter upon your inheritance, accept your responsibilities. ... Don't take 'no' for an answer. Never submit to failure. Do not be fobbed off with mere personal success or acceptance. You will make all kinds of mistakes; but as long as you are generous and true, and also fierce, you cannot hurt the world or even seriously distress her.

Winston Churchill said these inspiring words to a country at war, on the brink of disaster. He told the struggling people of England to challenge the status quo, to see the world as full of opportunities, to keep trying even when others may tell you to quit, to never indulge the self-doubt that comes from difficulties along the way, and, most of all, to approach life with generosity, truth, and passion. The world, Churchill reassures us, can handle our confidence.

For most of us, overcoming self-doubt is a difficult, life-long struggle.

Modern psychology aligns well with Pope's, Ford's, and Churchill's mandates. We have learned that the first step in developing confidence is to consciously identify the self-defeating thoughts that prevent us from being successful. The second step is to actively change these thought patterns and introduce new patterns that create positive results. Some of the typical negative thought patterns that we should be aware of include the following:

Perfectionism: The idea that if you are not perfect, you are a failure. This is "all or nothing" thinking, which keeps us from accepting ourselves and others as we are and from celebrating the progress that we've made. Perfectionism actually stems from arrogance: the belief that you can—and should—in fact be perfect. It is a refusal to accept your own inevitable limitations and to face the reality that you, like everyone else, make mistakes, and have the capacity for growth.

Pessimism: The belief that disaster lurks around every corner and that failure should be expected. This occurs when we diminish all the wonderful positive things that we have experienced and accomplished, and overemphasize the negative ones. This may stem from previous experiences in which we have been disappointed, leading us to believe that optimism is unrealistic. Pessimism, however, moves us to self-protective actions, leading to more fear and insecurity, less gratitude, and creating more pessimism.

Exaggeration: The tendency to increase or diminish the severity, importance, or meaning of an event or encounter (this is my automatic thought pattern, mentioned earlier). We exaggerate in order to feel more emotion by creating dramas, to avoid taking responsibility, or to dismiss the effort needed to seek a positive solution. It's easier to exaggerate than to carefully examine nuances and complexities.

Labeling: The wholesale categorization of a person or event. Labeling ignores the subtle differences that make every situation and individual unique and is usually employed to create division and conflict, and protect us from exploring aspects of ourselves that may be difficult, uncomfortable, or unflattering.

Difficulty Accepting Compliments: We may think that we are being humble when we brush aside or deflect a compliment, but we are actually rejecting a valuable gift and an opportunity to increase our confidence. We are also, consciously or unintentionally, diminishing the regard for the opinion of the one who gave us the compliment.

Jack Welch, the legendary CEO of General Electric, once said:

> *Confidence gives you courage and extends your reach. It lets you take greater risks and achieve far more than you ever thought possible.*

Welch, no stranger to swift and resolute action, and not one to readily take "no" for an answer, is telling us that once we embrace our own confidence, we will naturally take risks, and we will then discover that there are avenues to success that we did not even know existed. Of course, this is not an immediate or easy process and requires continual monitoring and updating. Again, there are specific strategies for developing confidence. The following list, which has been culled from many different sources, recommends some concrete actions. These include:

Focus on Your Strengths. Know where you are most effective, be comfortable with your inclinations and limitations, and allow yourself to be supported by others with complementary strengths. Develop what you do best. Why be mediocre at that which you are not inclined to do well, and don't enjoy doing, when you can be great at that which you naturally do well and enjoy? Remember that no one is complete enough to do all that is needed.

Take Risks. As Pope, Churchill, and Welch wrote, confident people take risks. Doing so opens you up to new possibilities and can increase your sense of adventure and fun, encouraging you to take more risks. This does not mean that you should be reckless, but that you should chance doing those uncomfortable or uncertain things that you know you should and find opportunities to challenge your pre-conceived sense of your own limitations.

Monitor Your Self-Talk. Catch yourself when you use negative self-talk, as discussed earlier. If you think positively and expect favorable results and

70

situations, in time your mental attitude will change how you view the events in your life. Even though the events themselves may not yet have changed, you will act with more positive energy and attract others with positive attitudes, thereby increasing your opportunities to succeed.

Visualize. When you visualize, you rehearse how a problem can be solved and how a new idea could be implemented. Visualization helps you to practice and to anticipate issues before they arise, leading to better performance and more confidence when the real thing occurs.

Evaluate Yourself Objectively. Learn to evaluate yourself independently and make adjustments without self-blame. Self-confidence is an attitude that allows individuals to have positive yet realistic views of themselves and their situations. Having self-confidence does not mean that individuals will be able to do everything, but self-confident people set expectations that are realistic based on their self-knowledge.

Give Yourself a Break. Most importantly (and, for many of us, the most difficult lesson), have compassion for yourself—as you would for others. We all stumble along the way and at times will feel insecure, unworthy, and disappointed. Embrace this as an inevitable component of the journey, which indicates that you are engaged and committed. Also, be sure to congratulate yourself on your accomplishments, which will increase your confidence.

Finally, the most moving and powerful quote on the topic of confidence was written by Marianne Williamson, in her book, *A Return to Love: Reflections on the Principles of a Course in Miracles*:

Our deepest fear is not that we are inadequate. Our deepest fear is that we are powerful beyond measure. It is our light, not our darkness that frightens us most. We ask ourselves, 'Who am I to be brilliant, gorgeous, talented, and famous?' Actually, who are you not to be? You are a child of God. Your playing small does not serve the world. There is nothing enlightened about shrinking so that people won't feel insecure around you. We were born to make manifest the glory of God that is within us. It's not just in some of us; it's in all of us. And when we let our own light shine, we unconsciously give other people permission to do the same. As we are liberated from our own fear, our presence automatically liberates others.

As Williamson teaches, confidence, at its deepest and most effective level, is the calm sense of your inherent goodness; that at your very essence, you are a product of the Source of all Goodness. Confidence is the belief that at their very essence, all others are also inherently good. And it is the knowledge that at its very essence, life—in all its abundance and complexity—is inherently good. With this confidence, you will naturally and readily embrace new opportunities and discover that confidence and success are your worthy gifts and inheritance.

Eureka!

Using Intuition

A legend that you might know:

A man takes a bath. He needs this bath because he is stressed, agitated, annoyed, and defeated. An important problem that he has been struggling to solve incessantly runs through his mind, calling to him for a solution. In spite of his best efforts, though, the solution eludes him—but the problem won't leave him alone. Finally, exhausted from the mental effort, he reluctantly decides to take a short bath before returning to his work. As he slides into the warm water, he begins to relax. He closes his eyes and feels the tension slowly drain from his forehead.

"Ah," he sighs, "just the break I need."

His arms and legs soften, and as his chest sinks into the water, he feels his hands gently float to the surface. He hears a light splash as water spills over the edge of the tub.

"I'll wipe up the water later," he thinks.

Suddenly, he sits upright. His eyes are wide, and a wild grin spreads across his face. He jumps out of the tub, and runs through the house.

"I have found it," he yells. "I have found it!"

"I must tell the king immediately," the man thinks, and so he runs out of the house toward the palace. His neighbors stare in shock at the wet, naked man, running up the cobblestone street, shouting, "I have found it!"

According to legend, the naked man was the ancient Greek mathematician Archimedes. His nagging problem: finding a way to determine if a crown that appears to be pure gold is in fact pure (the king, suspecting that the gold covers a copper base, hired the great Archimedes to confirm his suspicion). Legend tells us that while taking a bath, Archimedes suddenly realized that by measuring the amount of water that is displaced by an object (say, a gold crown), one can calculate its density, and hence its purity. In his excitement, he ran through the streets, shouting the now-familiar word, "Eureka!" ("I have found it" in Greek). This story is famous because it illustrates an important concept. At the moment when he stopped trying to solve the problem rationally and allowed unexpected wisdom to enter, Archimedes demonstrated the power of intuition.

Intuition is difficult to define, but we have all experienced it to some degree. Essentially, intuition is a faculty of knowing without the use of rational processes. Unlike typical *thinking*—which is a long, deliberate process—intuition is usually fast and unplanned.

At the moment when he stopped trying to solve the problem rationally and allowed unexpected wisdom to enter, Archimedes demonstrated the power of intuition.

And unlike the rational pursuit—which is linear in nature—intuitive insight typically arises from unexpected sources (like a bathtub). Intuitive insight most typically occurs when we are relaxed, open, and non-judgmental; when we are not actively looking for an answer. Intuition often results in a "eureka" moment, when we suddenly pass from not knowing to knowing, without knowing how we got there. This is an exciting, energizing moment, and like Archimedes, we may get caught up in the amazing discovery. We may find that we have lost track of time and place and may need some time to return to our normal state afterwards. This is because intuitive insight feels like a great unexpected gift.

For those who have difficulty with the concept of intuition, we can describe this phenomenon as an *inner voice*. We all have many voices in our heads competing for attention. There are voices of ambition, need, insecurity, anger, compassion, sabotage, fear, love, and so on. All these voices call to us at one time or another, depending on our emotional state and situation. Most of us are familiar with these voices, as though they are entities sitting on our shoulders whispering in our ears. Among all these voices, though, is one that has a special quality. It is wiser than we are. It is calmer. It is ego-less. It is objective. It is helpful. It is mistake-free. And it is consistent. When this voice calls, you may notice that your body relaxes, you experience an unusual mental clarity, and you feel a surge of energy. This is what the Bible calls the "still, small voice." This is the voice of intuition.

Where does intuitive insight come from? As you can guess, there are a myriad of proposed answers to this question. Depending on your paradigm, intuition might be one of the following:

- A normal action of the mind.
- Information from the collective consciousness.
- A result of a soul connection with the all-knowing Universe.
- An act of grace from a Higher Power.

We cannot know the answer, and perhaps all these are true in some way. What matters for us is the acknowledgment that intuition is a real phenomenon and that there are means to connect with this source of knowledge. Colin Powell, in *My American Journey*, notes his reliance on intuition:

> *Dig up all the information you can, then go with your instincts. We all have a certain intuition, and the older we get, the more we trust it…I use my intellect to inform my instinct. Then I use my instinct to test all this data. 'Hey, instinct, does this sound right? Does it smell right, feel right, fit right?'*

Another legend:

> *At the moment before a baby is born, it knows everything. It knows its purpose in this world. It knows what it is meant to accomplish, who it will meet, where it will go. It knows how the Universe operates. It knows everything because it is a pure, yet unborn soul, still connected to its Source. Albert Einstein and the Buddha are novices in comparison to this soon-to-be entity. At the very moment of its birth, an angel appears to the baby and places its heavenly finger under the baby's nose, creating the channel that connects nose to mouth. At that moment of the angel's touch, the baby instantly forgets everything and is a helpless, unknowing newborn, relying on the guidance and love of its parents and community. Yet all that it once knew remains, buried below the level of mind….*

This Yiddish fable, like all good legends, illustrates an existential truth with allegory and allusion. The existential truth: deep within us, we already know all that we need to know. This knowledge stays embedded somewhere in our psyche, and it is our responsibility to rediscover this knowledge through our own effort and choice. When we access this knowledge, then, we have a sudden "eureka" moment because we have found what we already knew to be true. When intuitive knowledge arrives, we—like Archimedes—immediately know that we have found the answer. We recognize that the insight is true, even though we have not processed it with our rational mind. We recognize it as true, even though it appeared as if from outside ourselves. We literally *recognize* the intuitive knowledge—we *recognize*, or *remember*.

The existential truth: deep within us, we already know all that we need to know.

Dr. Michael Ray, a professor at Stanford's MBA program, teaches intuition to business leaders. He has developed five truths about intuition that he has found can create powerful results when deliberately implemented. His five truths are:

1. **Intuition must be developed.** Each of us has intuition, but we must accept the responsibility for our individual style of intuition and its development. Although intuition is innate, for most of us this faculty has been muted by our reliance

on our intellect or emotions and requires that
we consciously work to reengage it.

2. **Intuition and reason are complementary.**
As Colin Powell wrote, reason and intuition are
not at odds but serve different, complementary
roles in the way that we receive and process
information.

3. **Intuition is unemotional.** It pays attention
clearly to the most appropriate alternative,
regardless of how we may feel about it (or
whose idea it may be). If there is ego-based
emotion or intellectual deliberation that accom-
panies the insight, it is probably not intuition.

4. **Intuition requires action.** Follow-through is
key to successful use of intuition and requires
consistent and deliberate effort. Intuition that is
not shared or implemented goes to waste.

5. **Intuition is mistake-free.** If we trust our
intuition, we will discover that it is always
aligned with the truth.

Successful people in any human endeavor rely
on intuition for guidance. Note, though, that the
reliance on intuition does not dismiss the need for
intellectual investigation. It is important to reiterate
that these are not opposing faculties and that we
are not "either-or" beings. We are not meant to dis-
regard intellect, but rather to seamlessly embrace
intuition and to use our intellect where it is most

effective—in gathering and analyzing facts. Peter Senge, in *The Fifth Discipline*, captured this idea eloquently:

> *People with high levels of personal mastery do not set out to integrate reason and intuition. Rather, they achieve it naturally—as a by-product of their commitment to use all the resources at their disposal. They cannot afford to choose between reason and intuition—or head and heart—any more than they would choose to walk on one leg or see with one eye.*

Intuition is one of the many arrows in our human quiver. It is always available, if we have the commitment to listen to its wisdom and the discipline and humility to accept and act upon its guidance.

I owe much of the insight on this subject to Lynn B. Robinson's excellent paper, Intuition in Business.

Something Creative

Accessing Creativity

For me, one of the pleasures and obligations of age and experience is the opportunity to offer career advice to young people and to help them find a job. This is very personally rewarding because it allows me to meet someone new, share what I've learned, and perhaps help another person in a substantial way. This is also professionally rewarding because it gives me a reason to call friends, colleagues, and clients who might be hiring and perhaps place someone in a position that could, frankly, be advantageous to me and my company. I recently met with a young woman who was looking for an entry-level job, and we spoke at length, discussing various options that she could pursue. During our conversation, I asked her a standard "interview question" that I have found reveals much about a person's attitudes and aspirations (and is a question that I regularly ask myself):

"Putting aside any perceived limitations," I said, "and allowing yourself to dream as big as you can, what would you most like to be doing for a livelihood five years from now?"

This is a huge, open-ended question that requires serious thought. Very quickly, though, she answered:

"I'm not exactly sure, but it would be something creative."

This was not an unusual response and is probably what I would have answered 25 years ago when, at her age, my most fervent dream was to be an artist. I had a very romantic image of the life of an artist and imagined myself in a shabby Soho loft, splattered with paint, standing before a large easel, valiantly suffering to birth painfully beautiful paintings that would shock and enlighten the world. This was my young, dramatic notion of a creative life. Of course, this is not how my life proceeded, and I could never have imagined that 25 years later, I'd be working for a large commercial real estate company, managing people and projects, tracking profit and loss sheets, and writing about issues of faith and religion. This was certainly not my idea of doing something creative! Now, though, I realize that my life is filled with creative opportunities in ways that are deeper, more nuanced, more challenging, and more satisfying than my youthful limited perspective could have conceived.

It is a common belief that creativity exists primarily in the realm of the arts. There is a glamour and status that surrounds the idea of being creative, as though the "creative person" contributes something of higher value than the average "worker." Like me, we may carry an image of the flamboyant

I realize that my life is filled with creative opportunities in ways that are deeper, more nuanced, more challenging, and more satisfying than my youthful limited perspective could have conceived.

genius, working alone, driven by the compulsion to create, producing works of music, painting, or literature that are at first condemned by the stifling pressure of convention, only later to be recognized as works of transcendent vision.

Creativity, we may think, is limited to the fringe artistic elite. This view, though, is a caricature of creativity that is actually a relatively recent invention, born from nineteenth-century Romanticism and its poetic conception of inspiration and genius. The etymology of the word "creativity" gives us a clearer insight into its deeper meaning. Its root is the Latin word *creatus*, which literally means "to have grown." Like gardening, creativity brings forth and nurtures something that already exists in its essence—in its seed—which lays hidden, waiting for us to find it and help it break through the surface to be revealed and to prosper. Creativity, then, is a natural process, not a mysterious state bestowed upon the gifted few. The Bible opens with the words:

In the beginning God created the heavens and the earth.

Creativity, the Bible tells us, is the first action of the Divine. That human beings are created in the "image" of God reminds us that our inherent impulse and highest calling is to create.

The creative process begins with a problem that one desires to solve and leads to the search for a solution. A creative solution is paradoxically both new and familiar. When a creative solution is found, our reaction is to say, "Of course!," as though we always knew, even though we just experienced it for the first time. Buckminster Fuller, the great dreamer, inventor, and philosopher, said of his process:

When I am working on a problem I never think about beauty. I only think about how to solve the problem. But when I have finished, if the solution is not beautiful, I know it is wrong.

For Fuller, a solution is beautiful because it is obviously right, and it is right because it is obviously beautiful. In this light, creativity is certainly not limited to the arts but includes any endeavor to discover an original, useful answer that lies beyond that which is readily apparent. So, it is possible to be a creative policeman; a creative scientist; a creative parent; even (gasp!), a creative businessperson.

For the last few decades, businesses have publicly touted creativity. We've heard that successful people can "think outside the box," and we too are encouraged to do so. There are many great companies that live this principle but, as many of

The creative process begins with a problem that one desires to solve and leads to the search for a solution. A creative solution is paradoxically both new and familiar.

us have experienced at some point in our careers, this principle may be touted but not rewarded. Of course, it is easy to blame the company, but if we honestly ask ourselves, "Was I truly trying to contribute to finding a solution, or was I looking for recognition, reward, or validation?" we might find a different culprit. This is because we may have only wanted to be perceived as being creative, which comes from feelings of personal need, instead of engaging in true creative thinking, which transcends the individual's ego, in search of a nonpersonal solution. Sincere creativity, we must know, is almost always welcomed.

Psychologists have studied creativity in order to help understand how the creative process operates.

Most agree that the key indicator of a person's capacity to be creative is the ability to quickly and confidently generate many possible diverse solutions, regardless of existing conventional answers. Linus Pauling, the only person to win Nobel prizes in two different fields, said:

> *The best way to have a good idea is to have lots of ideas.*

The essential attribute of a creative person, Pauling notes, is flexibility. And it seems that this ability is innate. I read a study that found that the average child thinks of 60 alternatives for any given situation. The study also found, however, that the average adult thinks of only 3–6 alternatives for the same situations. Although many of the child's ideas are fanciful, impractical, or unachievable, the child does not edit his responses and easily flows through various ideas without taking them personally and without preconceived limitations.

How, then, did the freedom of creative childhood become the limited thinking of the typical adult mind? The psychologist Abraham Maslow noted:

> *The key question isn't "What fosters creativity?" But it is why in God's name isn't everyone creative? Where was the human potential lost? How was it crippled?*

This crippling, it appears, attacks our flexibility. We slowly lose confidence in our own original ideas because we come to believe—or have been told—

that we should not challenge accepted answers or, perhaps, that we are not capable of doing so. In the process, we diminish our natural ability to be creative because we have limited our flexibility.

I recently heard an illuminating metaphor that describes how we can visualize this dynamic and help regain our flexibility. I attended a business seminar lead by a "futurist," who shared his vision of the way business will be conducted in the next decade or so. He began by contrasting the current situation to the way business was conducted in the past:

"When the large companies of the eighteenth and nineteenth century were established," he said, "the successful model was based on the idea of a trans-Atlantic voyage. Like this voyage, the business was created with a specific starting place and a known final destination. A plan was developed to get from point A to point B, and a ship—the business organization—was built, led by an omnipotent captain who directed all the activities of the shipmates, and whose word was law. He mapped the trip, assigned responsibilities, and launched to sea. The ship was built to be powerful and sturdy, but was not maneuverable or flexible because the destination was known and course corrections were not anticipated, or welcomed."

"Business today and in the future, however," the instructor said, "can't operate this way. Technology, culture, and society change too quickly to allow for such a rigid approach. By the time this ship has reached mid-ocean, the destination will have moved, changed, or vanished. The crew will become dissatisfied, frustrated, and lose motivation. Inevitably, the ship will run aground on an unexpected reef, or will simply drift aimlessly at sea."

"The new model," he said, "is not a trans-Atlantic ship, but is, instead, a whitewater raft. The world changes so quickly that we must now navigate a river rapid whose twists, turns, and accelerations obscure our view, and we cannot see very far in front of us. We cannot see where the river ultimately leads, and we cannot predict what is around the corner. In order to navigate such a river, we need to build a raft—the new business organization—to be light, flexible, able to quickly change directions, and manned by a crew that can handle many different responsibilities and work together in a team. At one moment, the oarsman in the right back must guide the raft. At another, the one on the left front. They must communicate quickly, and adapt to the changing situations. This model is not only much more effective than the old stodgy ship, it's also more exciting! Now, of course," the instructor noted, "you realize I am no longer talking only about business."

The whitewater raft is a model of creativity because the crew quickly and flexibly reacts to unexpected situations and the constant need to re-adjust the course. It is this inherent uncertainty—the need to find solutions in constant change—that builds flexibility and fosters creative solutions. Through this process, the crew develops competence, cooperation, communication, skill, confidence, and interdependency. This is what Martin Luther King referred to when he said:

Human salvation lies in the hands of the creatively maladjusted.

Those who creatively navigate life's whitewater challenges will feel a deep sense of personal accomplishment, which the sailors on the rigid ship, vainly attempting to stay on a bleak, stagnant linear trip, could not feel. This is because when we are immersed in true creativity, we feel powerfully engaged, and when we glimpse a creative solution, we feel a wonderful flush of energy that is both purposeful and liberating. Creativity, seen from this perspective, is our very nature and is available to us in everything that we do. It is not limited to a few people or select endeavors. We do not need to seek it, aspire to it, or dream of one day "being creative" or having a "creative job." We are creative when we freely and flexibly manifest the accessible, endless flow of creativity that imbues everything. And we can do that right now.

Do You Mean It?

Discovering Meaning

A friend, who is struggling to decide if he should stay in his current romantic relationship, asked if I would speak about the topic of commitment. I spent several days pondering the topic, asking myself such questions as:

- What do we mean when we say "I am committed to such and such?"
- Is a commitment a vow to stay involved with something—like a community, marriage, or job—and to never leave, in spite of circumstances?
- Is commitment simply a feeling that stems from the belief that something is important to us, and therefore we feel attached to it in some way?

- Are there obligations that go along with a commitment, and are there ways to measure whether we are fulfilling these obligations?
- Does the object of our commitment have any obligations to us?
- Are there circumstances in which it is appropriate to terminate the commitment?
- And finally, how do we decide what is worthy of our commitment?

These are not simple or light questions, to be sure. After several days of pondering these difficult questions, I could not find a point-of-entry to this topic that felt interesting, informative, personal, and true. I had only distilled the term *commitment* to this dry definition: "a duty or pledge to something or someone." Nothing new or interesting there. As I was ready to shelve this topic for another time and consider a different subject for the upcoming Monday morning meeting, I decided to focus for a moment on what seemed to be the most important of the questions: "How do we decide what is worthy of our commitment?" This is the key question, it seemed to me, because we may believe that if we commit to the wrong thing or person, all our dedication and energy might be wasted.

"How do we decide what is worthy of our commitment?"

Perhaps this explains "commitment phobia." We all know a person with this condition: one who is unwilling to commit (say, to a relationship or career) for fear that he may someday discover that he has made a mistake and that other options may have been better choices. Because of this fear, such a person drifts from one thing to another and from one person to another. Without commitment, he will never establish rewarding relationships with others. Without commitment, he will never undertake anything truly important, lasting, or rewarding. Ultimately, without commitment, his life won't have significant meaning.

The deceptively simple answer to the question, "How do we decide what is worthy of our commitment?" then, is that we must commit to something that is meaningful—something that gives us a sense of purpose. Meaning and purpose—now that's an interesting aspect of commitment worthy of exploration! Certainly the most basic of all philosophical questions are: "Why am I here?" "What is the meaning of my life?" and "What is the purpose for my time on earth?" Try as we might to ignore these essential questions, as human beings we seem to have an innate desire to find the answers. We crave meaning and purpose.

The best-selling book in the world in 2003, 2004, and 2005 was a small devotional book that addressed this human craving for meaning and purpose. Titled *The Purpose Driven Life*, this book has sold over 25 million copies and is the best-selling hardback book in American history. Written by Christian minister Rick Warren, this book provides a 40-day process to help readers identify and live their own purpose. The title of the first chapter, *What on Earth Am I Here For?*, indicates the book's lofty ambition. Warren preaches a powerful, essential, and resonant message: We are here for a purpose. It is through commitment to this purpose, Warren argues, that we lead meaningful, rewarding, fulfilling, and helpful lives.

This idea, that we thrive when we have committed to a meaningful purpose, is not a new one. In the 1950s, psychologist Viktor Frankl built a new branch of psychotherapy around the notion that mental health is a result of living a life dedicated to meaning. Frankl was a concentration camp prisoner who survived by finding meaning in his life, even in the midst of incomprehensible despair, inhumanity, brutality, torture, and death. In his book, *Man's Search for Meaning*, Frankl explains the origins of his approach:

> *At the beginning of human history, man lost some of the basic animal instincts in which an animal's behavior is imbedded, and by which it is secured. Such security, like Paradise, is closed to man forever; man has to make choices. In addition to this, however, man has suffered*

another loss in his more recent development inasmuch as the traditions which buttressed his behavior are now rapidly diminishing. No instinct tells what he has to do, and no tradition tells him what he ought to do; sometimes he does not even know what he wishes to do. Instead, he either wishes to do what other people do (conformism) or he does what other people wish him to do (totalitarianism).

Frankl believed, therefore, that we must consciously choose to discover and commit to a purpose beyond our desire for conformity or subservience. Frankl taught that only by committing to "The Will to Meaning" can we lead healthy lives. Frankl's mentor, the famous psychologist and philosopher Carl Jung, made a similar observation in the 1920s:

About one-third of my cases are suffering from no clinically definable neurosis, but from the senselessness and emptiness of their lives. This can be described as the general neurosis of our time.

How do we discover our purpose and commit to a meaningful life? Frankly, there does not seem to be a quick answer to this question. Warren, Frankl, Jung, and others who have embraced meaningful purpose as life's goal have all made the same observation: We each have our own unique and individual purpose, and the discovery of that purpose is our life's journey, for which we must take personal responsibility. There is a clue, however, that might help point us in the right direction. Warren refers to *The Purpose Driven Life* as an "anti self-help book." He makes this clear in the very first sentence, by stating bluntly, "It's not about you." Here, then, is the paradoxical truth: In order to find personal meaning and purpose, we must first learn to put our own personal needs aside.

In case you are tempted to think this is simply an abstract spiritual process with little or no real-world application, all you need to do is read the book that seems to be on every successful businessperson's bookshelf: *Good to Great* by Jim Collins. In this book, Collins presents the findings of his in-depth, five-year investigation on what makes companies great. He investigated companies that routinely grow at rates far in excess of the market and provide superior products and services. Collins discovered that *great* begins at the top—with the company's leader—and outlines the qualities of successful leaders by ranking them on a scale of 1–5. The Level 1 leader is the "Highly Capable Individual" who "makes productive contributions through talent, knowledge, skills, and good work habits." This is the lowest-level leader—one who competently does his or her job, and that's it. At the top is the Level 5 Executive—the "Great Leader." Collins describes such an individual:

Level 5 leaders channel their ego away from themselves and into a larger goal of building a great company. It's not that Level 5 leaders have no ego or self-interest. Indeed, they are incredibly ambitious—but their ambition is first and foremost for the institution, not themselves.

For the great leader, then, it's not about them—it's about their purpose. This mirrors Warren's opening statement, "It's not about you." Collins also notes that these leaders create committed nurturing relationships with their teams and that these leaders stay committed to their purpose through the inevitable challenges and naysayers. Frankl discovered the same essential truth and describes three principles that help us to get outside of ourselves in order to direct us toward a life of purpose and meaning:

1. We must commit to create something or do something.

2. We must commit to loving relationships with others.

3. We must commit to accepting the unavoidable suffering that is an inevitable part of life.

Frankl's process sounds very simple but contains the essential array of commitments. With these, we naturally find meaning because we discover that meaning and purpose actually arise from commitment to positive action, to love, and to life, in all its unfolding. Commitment energizes and sustains our search for purpose and meaning, which increases commitment, enriching meaning, and deepening our sense of purpose. This is our fondest yearning. Harold Kushner, in *When All You Ever Wanted Is Not Enough*, beautifully sums this up :

> *Our souls are hungry for meaning, for the sense that we have figured out how to live so that our lives matter, so that the world will be at least a little different for our having passed through it.*

You're Finished!

Embracing Change

There was once a philosophy professor who opened each class by reminding his students that the true test of any philosophical belief is whether that belief is itself paradoxical. In other words, the belief must be internally self-contradictory. This is a difficult concept to grasp, so one of his students approached a math professor and asked if he could explain this puzzling teaching. The math professor came to the next class, and as the philosophy professor was about to begin, stood and asked,

"Sir, do you really believe that all truth is based on paradox?"

The philosophy professor scratched his head and thoughtfully answered,

"Well, yes… and no."

I'd like to offer such a paradoxical statement by the ancient Greek philosopher Heraclitus:

There is nothing permanent except change.

Change is inevitable. The very workings of the Universe and of all life is based on change. As we currently understand it, the Universe itself began with the most massive change imaginable: an infinitely paradoxical (how can something emerge from nothing?), infinitely hot, infinitely fast explosion from an infinitely small particle that resulted in the creation of all time and matter. Since that moment, 15 billion years ago, everything has been in constant change. Matter coalesces into stars and planets and develops into life, as the Universe continues to expand toward an unknowable, incredibly distant future. All life as we know it is based on change, since all growth is a product of change. Cells are born, grow, and die, as new ones take their place. Without change, there is no life because without change, there is no growth. The process of evolution is based on the notion that periodic, often dramatic changes occur, leading to the creation of new, more advanced species that further the progress of intelligence and diversity. Charles Darwin himself noted this succinctly:

It is not the strongest of the species that survives, nor the most intelligent, but the one most responsive to change.

Change, then, is built into the very fabric of our existence. And the opposite of change is decay, and ultimately, death. Benjamin Franklin cleverly stated (a century before Darwin):

When you're finished changing, you're finished.

Although change is inevitable and is the vehicle for growth and progress, it is important to note that there are different types of change. First, there are the expected changes that routinely occur in our lives: the change of seasons, the aging of our bodies, the growth of our children, minor illnesses, wear and tear of our possessions, and the ubiquitous late train and traffic jam that changes our schedule. These changes usually occur slowly, with some level of predictability. For most of us, these changes are anticipated, and we face them with a mixture of humor, frustration, and resignation, depending upon our inclination and the nature of the change.

Second, there are the sudden, dramatic, or unexpected changes that can seem to come out of nowhere, catch us unprepared, or shake our sense of security. These can be changes that we perceive as good, such as the birth of a child, marriage, a new job, a new house in a new city, or our children's graduations; and changes that we usually perceive as bad, such as being fired from a job, experiencing a divorce, losing a longtime friendship, or, God forbid, the passing of a friend or family member. Whether we perceive these changes as good or bad, they are difficult and can produce stress and anxiety.

This second kind of change is the type that we struggle with and that causes us pain. Such changes can be frightening, intimidating, and unsettling. Many of us avoid these changes, or we may hunker down, pretend that nothing is happening, and hope that it will pass over us and go away. "Why is this happening to me?" we may ask. Or maybe we complain, "I didn't see this one coming. How come things can't stay the same as they were?" In his groundbreaking book, *The Road Less Traveled*, psychiatrist M. Scott Peck points out that the reason this type of change is so difficult for many of us is because these changes force us out of our comfort zone and require us to rethink the internal map that we've created for how we think things are and ought to be.

This rethinking can be very painful because it may result in the conclusion that some of our dearly held beliefs may need modification, or outright rejection. It can also be painful because it may require us to have the discipline and energy to address the change and to fight our inherent laziness and aversion to action. In either case, such changes force us to look inward and to make an honest assessment of our beliefs and our habits and to accept the basic fact that everything will inevitably change. As the mid-twentieth century Zen Buddhist priest Shunryu Suzuki taught:

> *Without accepting the fact that everything changes, we cannot find perfect composure. But unfortunately, although it is true, it is difficult for us to accept it. Because we cannot accept the truth of transience, we suffer.*

Because change is not only inevitable, but is, in fact, the essential vehicle for growth, how do we embrace the sudden, dramatic, and often unexpected changes? As Peck noted, we must have the confidence and strength to look at the situation as honestly as possible, assess where previously held beliefs are keeping us from growing, and muster the energy to implement a new course of action. In essence, these external changes result in our own internal change and are the catalysts for personal growth. We all know people (and we may be one ourselves) who faced an unexpected event that was completely unwelcome when it occurred, but who now look back on that event as a key turning point in their lives. Through addressing this event, that person experienced growth that might not have happened otherwise. This is what is meant by the famous, often-quoted truism:

As a door closes, a window opens.

Although it may be a tight squeeze, by going through that window, we discover a landscape of possibilities that we may never had known existed if the same old door that we had been walking through all of our lives had not suddenly been closed. In this light, change is a gift that presents opportunity for growth.

Last week, my wife and I rewatched one of her favorite movies, *Parenthood*, the 1989 comedy about the challenges of raising children. This movie follows

the lives of several genera-
tions of one family and
shows different attitudes
and styles of parenting.
One of the parents, played
by Steve Martin, is a man
who is devoted to his wife
and children. He tries hard
to meet their various physical and psychological
needs and is alert to the

*Changes force us to
look inward and to
make an honest
assessment of our
beliefs and our
habits, and to accept
the basic fact that
everything will
inevitably change.*

need to balance his responsibilities at work and at
home. In spite of all his efforts, though, he cannot
control the changes that happen around him. Finally,
in a fit of frustration, he cries,

"I don't have choices, only obligations!"

His unflappable live-in grandmother overhears
his outburst and calmly says to him,

"Some people like the merry-go-round. I always
preferred the roller coaster. It's more exciting."

At the time, he has no idea what she means and
dismisses her comment as an unintelligible senior
outburst. By the end of the movie, after all his
images of how his life should be collapse, he understands her advice. He learns that life is inevitably
filled with the unexpected roller coaster drops, turns,

accelerations, and climbs, and that although he can prefer that things keep going around in an expected way, not only is this not realistic, it's no fun! When he lets go of the need to control change, and sees life as an ever-changing thrill ride, he and his family begin to relax, and each one prospers in their own specific way.

It is important to point out that not all changes are to be embraced and encouraged. Change must be approached maturely and sensitively, with a focus on positive growth. Certainly it is not good to change jobs, careers, houses, or spouses every year. Such constant change is an avoidance of responsibility and commitment. Often, when it is within our hands, stability should be encouraged. There are also events that happen to us that seem to have no ready explanation or redeeming purpose and from which the best we can do is try to endure. But when we embrace the inevitable changes in our lives, we can grow in new, exciting, rewarding directions that we never could have planned. The final word on the paradox of change, which is attributed to St. Francis of Assisi, contains the simple, powerful prayer:

> *God grant me the serenity to accept the things I cannot change, the courage to change the things I can, and the wisdom to know the difference.*

I owe much of the insight in this chapter to my wife, Shirona.

Alone on the Sofa

Finding Truth

In the previous chapter, titled "You're Finished," I mentioned that, in some way, all profound truths are inherently paradoxical. The example given was, "The only constant is change." Of course, there are many other well-known paradoxes, such as, "Only by giving to others do we ultimately receive." Or "The more we know, the more we know we don't know." Or "The best way to heal our egos is to practice letting go of the needs of the ego." These are complex universal truths. If we look carefully, we discover that even truth itself is inherently paradoxical. Simply stated:

> *Truth itself is absolutely objective, and absolutely subjective.*

This is perhaps the ultimate paradox because the truth, we may believe, is ultimately fixed, measurable, and knowable: The Earth orbits the Sun,

George Washington was America's first president, I was born in Brooklyn, five times five equals twenty-five. We know that we should tell the truth. We know that we should not lie because lying leads to corruption, damaged relationships, and spiritual decline. This is all absolutely correct. "Don't lie" (bear false witness) is one of the Ten Commandments, along with the other moral commandments, such as "don't murder" and "don't steal." On the other hand, we know that there are many things that were considered true in the past that we now know to be false (gee, the earth sure seemed flat!). We also know that something that is absolutely true to one person is often another's preference, falsehood, or myth. Finally, we might have discovered that there are times in which telling some, or all, of the truth, as we perceived it, should be avoided. So we are left with two questions: "What is truth?" and "What is the moral imperative to tell the truth?"

These questions have been at the essence of a philosophical debate begun 2,500 years ago by the great Greek philosophers. They believed, quite

> *We might have discovered that there are times in which telling some, or all, of the truth, as we perceived it, should be avoided.*

reasonably, that we say something is true when our knowledge of it corresponds to the measurable fact of the thing. Thomas Aquinas, the medieval Christian theologian, reiterated that truth is simply "the conformity of the intellect to the thing." Later philosophers argued, however, that truth is, in reality, often fluid and nuanced. Perhaps something is only known to be true, they said, when it is agreed to be so by a majority of people or when it addresses the higher good of society as a whole. Truth, others argued, actually varies dramatically from person to person depending on cultural upbringing or inclination. Of course, the Earth remains in orbit around the Sun, but my individual experiences and perceptions create a personal reality that may have little in common with any general consensus or with anyone else's reality. Now, quantum physics seems to have found that, at the most fundamental level, time and matter only come into existence when an observer participates in the process of creation. The perspective of the observer colors the object and event being viewed, creating a subjective reality that, to the observer, appears as an objective truth.

Now we return to the original questions: "Can we define truth?" and "How should we tell the truth?" Consider the following scenes:

Scene 1

(Feel free to reverse roles/genders or modify the details to match your experience.)

It is evening. You are at home, sitting alone on the sofa. Your wife comes down the stairs and hurries over to you. You notice that she is wearing a new dress and that there is a big, happy grin on her face. "Honey," she calls excitedly, "don't you love this new dress?" She swivels slowly, so you can get a good look. When she turns to you for your opinion, you scan the dress and honestly answer, "I don't like it. The color is too dark, the print is fussy, and it doesn't fit you well. As a matter of fact, I don't really care for most of the clothing in your wardrobe." The grin quickly vanishes from her face. You spend the night sleeping alone on that sofa.

Consider this alternate ending:

When she turns to you for your opinion, you look at her, and see how happy she is—the woman that you love—and you honestly answer. "I have never seen you look so beautiful, sweetheart. You look wonderful." Her smile broadens. You arrive to work late the next morning, tired but happy.

Scene 2

(And, as before, feel free to modify the details to match your experience.)

You arrive 15 minutes late to a business meeting with a client because you needed to answer an important phone call, which you received just as you were ready to leave for the meeting. Your client asks, "What kept you?" You look at him and honestly answer, "Another client with a much bigger project than yours called, and I decided it was better to be late to your meeting than to miss her call. And, by the way, she pays her bills faster than you do." The client excuses himself to make a phone call to your boss. You begin updating your resume.

Consider this alternate ending:

Your client stands up and asks, "What kept you?" You look at him and notice that he is anxious and concerned—a client who needs your help—and you honestly answer: "Please forgive me. I'm sorry to have kept you waiting. Something unexpected came up as I was leaving that needed my attention. Now, how can I help you?" You listen carefully as he explains his issue. You stay late to help him resolve his problem. Later, you ponder how to spend your larger-than-expected bonus.

In these examples, truth was viewed from different angles. Of course, no one (we hope) would be so blunt as to answer according to the first endings, but these first answers were, in fact, the truth. So were the reconsidered answers. There's the paradox. In both endings, you tell the truth, but with very different intents and results. The difference is the choice that you make. Is this to say that truth is always subjective? As stated at the beginning, the answer must be yes and no. Unless one is a criminal, we can all agree that lying is wrong. People devoted to humanity must agree that murder and stealing are absolutely wrong. We must agree that freedom and health are good, and slavery and abuse are bad. On the other hand, horrific wars of political ideology and intransigent theology waged by opposing sides— each convinced that their side is true—teach us that absolute certainty can be very dangerous and must be challenged. To believe that there is no absolute truth, though, can be as dangerous as to believe that there is only one truth to which you adhere. But without a belief in absolute truth, morality is merely a temporary, convenient agreement. This can make your head spin!

How can we navigate this complex reality? As the earlier scenes demonstrated, we must be careful how, when, and why we speak a truth. In the first approach, you bluntly and coldly tell your truth of the situation, without thought to the feelings of the other person or the consequences of your words. The result is hurtful to the other, detrimental to you, and does not serve any larger purpose. In the reconsidered answers, you are equally devoted to the truth. This is not ingratiating or pandering. The answers were absolutely true, but before speaking, you consciously elevated yourself to a higher truth—a truth that encompasses the needs of the other, that sees the situation from a broader perspective, and that creates positive results.

This is the objective and subjective paradox of truth. The resolution is found in the dedication to seeking, speaking, and acting on a unified truth that is both personally sincere, yet sensitive to others, promoting spiritual development for all. In his book, *You Shall Be Holy*, Joseph Telushkin lists several instances in which we should be silent or when our impulse to tell the blunt truth may be put aside in order to serve a higher purpose:

- To prevent future harm (when your life or another's is at stake).
- To right a wrong or past wrong done to you (when dealing with a dishonest person).
- To prevent unnecessarily hurting someone's feelings.
- To create peace or do good (smoothing over conflicts between friends or lying to a poor person so that he will accept charity).
- To maintain privacy (not telling personal details that embarrass you or another).
- To make a point or elucidate an opinion (consciously using allegory or exaggeration to illuminate an idea).

If we agree that the pursuit of truth is essential and that telling the truth is a noble endeavor, we are called to continually struggle to find our way, to challenge our position, and to speak the highest truth from the loftiest perspective. We learn that there are instances in which we must question our preconceived sense of what's true and allow room for another person's views and feelings to enter. This is a difficult challenge and defies simple, ready answers. But, of course, nobody said that paradoxes are easy.

THE SUPERIOR OBJECT

RESOLVING CONFLICTS OF INTEREST

Consider the following scenarios:

Scenario 1: *A new potential client calls to ask you to come in for an interview for a significant project. You are currently providing similar services to another company that is their direct competition. You believe that the new potential client does not know about this, and you suspect that if they knew, they might not hire you. You tell yourself:*

"Since our work is confidential, it is unlikely that either side will ever know. Besides, working for competing companies is standard practice in the market today."

Should you go to the interview?

Scenario 2: *You work for a small company and are responsible for procuring construction services. You recently received bids from several contractors and are reviewing their numbers. Among the bidders is a company whose president is a professional acquaintance, and his bid is slightly above the lowest bidder. You had been hoping to* *build a relationship with this person because you feel that it would be good for your career, and you have even been considering approaching this person about a job. You tell yourself:*

"I know that they will do good work. Plus, their bid wasn't that much higher anyway."

No one will question your decision. Who should you hire?

Scenario 3: *You specialize in working on large corporate headquarters projects, and you recently received a request for proposal from a major company who manufactures a product that you believe is detrimental to the public's health. This project is right up your alley, though, and would supply enough fees to meet your revenue targets, and perhaps even allow you to add new staff. You have been teaching your children about the dangers of this company's product, but this is an enormous opportunity. You tell yourself:*

"Who am I to judge what my clients do? I need this project, and, besides, if I don't take this job, someone else will."

Do you answer the proposal?

You may have found some of these scenarios to be familiar, or perhaps you have struggled with similar dilemmas. Chances are, though, that you have been exposed to the common factor that all these scenarios share: They pose conflicts of interest. The first is a professional conflict, the second is a personal conflict, and the third is a moral conflict.

A conflict of interest can be defined as:

A situation in which someone in a position of trust has competing professional or personal interests. Such competing interests can make it difficult to fulfill his or her duties impartially.

In this post-Enron, Sarbanes-Oxley era, most companies have implemented codes of ethics that address such conflicts of interest and spell out appropriate responses to specific conflicts, along with repercussions for failure to comply—ranging from reprimand to termination and criminal investigation. This has raised the awareness of these issues and has increased due diligence to make sure that such conflicts are avoided.

I've looked at several "conflict of interest" policies in preparation for these remarks and have found that many of the conflicts of interest discussed are *obviously* immoral, unethical, or illegal. Does a politician really need to be told that it's wrong to receive personal gifts from lobbyists? Does a lawyer really need to be told that it's wrong to represent a party with interests adverse to those of a current client? Does a businessperson really need to be told that it's wrong to share company secrets for personal gain or to hire an unqualified friend or family member? Other examples, though, like the ones I gave in the beginning, may not have such obvious answers. So what do we do when such unclear conflicts arise?

The typical responses to conflicts of interest usually involve one of the following three actions:

1. Removal
2. Recusal
3. Disclosure

You can simply *remove* the conflict by setting up a mechanism in which the conflict no longer exists, you can *recuse* yourself from participating in the conflict, or you can openly *disclose* the conflict and let the involved parties decide how to proceed. All of these actions have one crucial element in common: They all begin with the recognition that a conflict exists and that it must be addressed honestly and openly. They also begin with the desire to be honest and to tell the truth about the conflict of interest.

> *Begin with the recognition that a conflict exists, and that it must be addressed honestly and openly.*

But why do we need to be *told* to be honest? Why is honesty often so difficult? In the preceding examples, honesty seems to be at odds with financial success. If the first person discloses that he is working for the competitor, he may not win the job. If the second person gives the job to the low bidder (or recuses himself from the decision), she may miss the opportunity to advance her career. If the third person turns down the job for moral reasons, he may have to reduce his staff or miss making his revenue target. Honesty seems to be at war with winning and success. It's like the cartoon image of the man with an angel on one shoulder and a devil on the other, each whispering in his ear. In this cartoon, the man ultimately kicks the angel to the curb because the other voice offers more tangible reward and satisfaction.

Is this a real model, though? Are honesty and success actually at odds? Consider any people that you respect and trust, whether in your personal or business life. Undoubtedly, the significant characteristic of these people is honesty. You trust and respect them because you know that you can rely on them to tell you the truth. We have all read of "flashes-in-the-pan"—those who made quick fortunes but were soon discovered to have cut corners, made backroom deals, or to have cheated outright. These people quickly fade because their credibility is undermined by their unscrupulous actions. People who consistently and clearly tell the truth, however, build trust, which results in a good reputation, which begets new and repeat clients, which increases business, which accumulates success and wealth.

Spiritual teachings recognize this mechanism: that honesty ultimately leads to success. The Book of Proverbs, the collection of wisdom teachings about living a good life, states:

> *Truthful lips endure forever, but a lying tongue lasts only a moment…The hand of the diligent will rule, but deceit will melt.*

A lie may bring short-term results, but it is only through the commitment to truth that long-term success is built. This spiritual teaching directly links honesty to success and provides the simple answer to conflicts of interest: *Tell the truth*. It may mean turning away the immediate financial reward, but it will keep you out of trouble, and practiced with diligence, honest disclosure will actually lead to future prosperity.

The question remains: Why be tempted to engage in conflicts of interest? Why not simply tell the truth? As the scenarios at the beginning of this chapter pointed out, the truth may not always be readily apparent. We can all too easily play mind games; convince ourselves that there is no conflict, that it's okay to follow a path that we suspect may not be honest. "Everyone else does it," we may think, or maybe we'll convince ourselves that it's not really all that bad. The conflict of interest is essentially between honesty and deceit. Here, we find that the commitment to truth must start with the courage to deeply examine our motives and ask ourselves if we are being, first and foremost, honest to ourselves. This requires the strength to look squarely at the answer, face our own inclination to deny or distort our intentions, and the confidence to know that honesty is indeed the best policy.

Confucius, in his usual pithy, wise, and brief manner, sharply sums up this subject by noting:

The object of the superior person is truth.

I owe much of the insight in this message to my friend and colleague, Marcus Raynor.

HEY, YOU SCREWED UP AGAIN!

TRANSFORMING MISTAKES

I have a confession. A few weeks ago, I made a mistake—a real honest-to-goodness screw-up. I told a client that, based on my recent experiences on a similar project, an important piece of equipment that is needed for their project would require a nine-month lead time, putting its delivery well beyond the project deadline. Based on this advice, the client became very concerned, passed my information to his boss, and we began to look for other options that could meet their goals. A week later, though, I received a call from the general contractor, who told me that he researched the issue and found that this piece of equipment can actually be delivered in four months, well within the project schedule. This was good for the project, but frustrating for the client, and personally embarrassing for me.

I don't know about you, but when I make a mistake, whether it's at work (like the preceding example), at home, at sports, or, I must admit, practically anywhere, my first reaction is often to be very harsh on myself. "You screwed up again!" that inner voice yells. "You should have known better! How could you have done that?" In the words of the great late-twentieth century existential philosopher, Britney Spears:

Oops, I did it again!

Another great philosopher addressed this issue 3,000 years earlier in The Book of Ecclesiastes, when the author—traditionally identified as King Solomon—says,

No one is so perfect that he has never sinned.

This seems to be a very obvious statement (any perfect people here?), but this is a necessary starting point as an acknowledgment of the basic truth that we all know: Everyone makes mistakes.

But wait a minute, the text says "sin," not "mistake." Isn't there a big difference between these words? The word *sin* often carries the connotation of a deliberate religious or spiritual transgression, whereas *mistake* is a mundane term that refers to everyday unintentional human error. This is only an English distinction, however, because in Hebrew—the language of Ecclesiastes—the word for sin, *chait* (the *"ch"* is pronounced as an "h" sound from the back of the throat), literally means *missing the mark*. In other words, a sin occurs when we do not aim our intentions and actions at the right target, or when we do want to aim correctly but are off target in what we do and say. The original intention of the word "sin" is actually very close in meaning to a *mistake*, or a wrong action.

What *mark* or *take*, though, are we missing? Is the mark perfection? Ecclesiastes emphatically answers "no." As human beings, we will inevitably make mistakes. The target is the acceptance of our basic humanness; that although we are fallible, we were given the ability to grow through the conscious choices that we make, and that we are created in the image of the Divine, capable of grace, kindness, compassion, and the experience of transcendence.

What do we do, then, when a mistake occurs? Are mistakes simply inevitable nuisances that must be accepted and endured? With experience and guidance, we discover that mistakes can, in fact, often be turned around and transformed into a positive growth experiences. When properly handled, mistakes provide a means to identify areas that need attention, improve our skills, deepen our relationships, and open new avenues that may have otherwise remained hidden. There are many famous examples of such turn-arounds, from Columbus accidentally discovering the New World while searching for a trade route to the East, to Edison's discovery of the correct light bulb filament after thousands of "mistakes."

While recently watching a TV show on the History Channel, I learned of a wonderful mistake that resulted in a product that almost everyone will know. In 1943, Richard James, a naval engineer, was conducting an experiment to create tension springs to absorb equipment impact in ships. His spring was a failure and buckled under the machine stress. During one experiment, though, the spring jumped from the table, fell to the floor, sprung to a nearby stair, and to James's amazement, it began to "walk" down the stair by itself. James showed this to his wife, who immediately recognized an idea for a toy in her husband's failed tension spring. The toy debuted in 1945 at Gimbel's Department Store in Philadelphia. Since then, more than 300 million of James's failed naval tension springs, the iconic *Slinky*, have sold worldwide.

With experience and guidance, we discover that mistakes can, in fact, often be turned around and transformed into a positive growth experience.

So instead of yelling at ourselves, "Hey, you screwed up again!" we can see a mistake as an opportunity for growth. Most wisdom traditions and effective business practices, not to mention common sense, have a system for facilitating this transformation. Buddhists call this process, "turning arrows in to flower petals," or "turning poison into good food." Judaism calls this process *t'shuvah*, which literally means "returning;" returning to the awareness of who we are through re-aiming at the right target. This process begins with an essential first step: Take responsibility! Recognize and admit that a mistake has been made, and avoid attempting to hide it, deny it, or blame others. Without this essential first step, the process stalls, and we close ourselves off to any growth potential.

After taking this crucial internal first step—accepting responsibility without self-blame and without blaming others—the next step is a very physical one: We must fix the mistake. This may require anything from a simple apology, to monetary compensation, or a dramatic change in our behavior. After this, we must determine to learn from the mistake and not repeat it in the future. When this process is followed, the inevitable mistake can be embraced and even viewed as a positive experience. To drive home the point, here are a few famous quotes about the nature of mistakes:

Oscar Wilde: *Experience is simply the name we give our mistakes.*

Mahatma Gandhi: *Freedom is not worth having if it does not include the freedom to make mistakes.*

Albert Einstein: *Anyone who has never made a mistake has never tried anything new.*

George Bernard Shaw: *While one person hesitates because he feels inferior, the other is busy making mistakes and becoming superior.*

By now, you may be wondering: How did my mistake turn out? After deciding to stop beating myself up for having made a mistake, I called the contractor, and we met to review the information he found. We then developed a joint approach to inform the client, who was actually very relieved and grateful that we found an answer to his problem. He also said that he appreciated that we were working as a team and that we candidly identified a problem and fixed it. Now, my relationship is stronger with the contractor, the owner has seen a problem-solving process in action, and you can be sure that before mentioning lead times in this volatile equipment market, I will more thoroughly research the issue in advance.

In retrospect, this was a very small mistake—a minor *sin*—(I've made bigger mistakes, of course, but my boss might be reading this) but the process worked. Now, of course, we should try to avoid mistakes whenever possible. But when the inevitable mistake does occur, instead of shouting to ourselves, "You screwed up again!" or, conversely, telling ourselves that this is not our fault, or someone else is to blame, and that there is nothing to be done to fix it, we can use this simple process to repair the damage, learn from it, and move forward. Imagine taking this process into your most difficult business deals, your most intimate personal relationships, or perhaps even with the stranger on the train, on whose toe you inadvertently stepped.

Making Stuff Up

Reacting Objectively

Over the last 15 years or so I have participated in many religious classes, retreats, and personal development workshops, in search of transformational spiritual insights and practices that I can teach and put to use. In retrospect, one of the most powerful spiritual lessons that I've learned, though, came from a business management seminar that I attended several years ago. The focus of this seminar was the usual material that one would expect: ways to increase productivity, control costs, exceed client expectations, and improve the work product. Toward the end of the seminar the instructor suddenly made an unexpected remark:

"In spite of where you attended college, what you do for a living, or your position in your company, you are all graduates from MSU—Making Stuff Up (well, she didn't actually use the word "Stuff").

Most of you walk around thinking that you know what's happening, that you comprehend the dynamics of a situation, and that you understand why people do what they do. You act on these premises and think that you are simply responding to the events and people around you. I will guarantee to you, though, that most of this is not as objective as you may think and that, in fact, most of it is stuff that you made up."

To demonstrate this, the instructor asked a young man sitting in the front row to come up on stage. She asked him to imagine that he was a new, entry-level employee at a large company where she (the instructor) was the CEO.

"Now, imagine," she said, "that we are about to pass each other in a corridor. When we pass I'd like you to say 'Good morning, Ms. Jones.' That's it."

The two went to opposite ends of the stage and walked toward each other. As they passed, the young man said,

"Good morning, Ms. Jones."

The instructor looked straight ahead, kept walking, and said nothing. After a moment, she asked him,

"Okay, how did that make you feel?"

"Lousy," he said.

"Why?" she asked.

"Because you deliberately ignored me," he said.

"I *deliberately* ignored you? Why do you think that?" she asked.

"Because you didn't even respond when I said 'hello,'" he answered.

"And *why* do you think that I didn't respond?" she prompted him.

"Probably because you think that you are an important person and I'm not" he said, now, visibly upset. "You acted as though I didn't even exist. As though you are better than me."

"But you just *assumed* my reason for not answering is because I think I'm better than you," she said. "What if I told you that I'm hard of hearing, or that I'm shy around new people, or that I didn't remember your name and was embarrassed, or that, heaven forbid, something terrible had happened in my personal life and I was distracted. There are dozens of possible reasons why I didn't say 'hi,' yet you assumed it was because I thought little of you. Now you are angry and frustrated, and you made it all up! You demonstrated MSU in action."

We do all seem to be graduates of MSU. How often have you seen an event, quickly determined the motives of those involved, passed judgment, and left feeling angry, hurt, or disappointed? How often have you looked back on these events, only to realize that you were wrong? The stranger who you thought was arrogant actually turned out to be a very nice guy with a dry sense of humor; the friend who didn't respond to your email actually got a new address and never received it; the business acquaintance who left you off his bid list was acting on the direction of the client and didn't know how to tell you. The stuff that we make up can be very damaging. In personal life and in business, this stuff can hurt relationships, keep us from developing new opportunities, and simply make our lives less happy and less productive. For many of us, making stuff up is second nature. We make stuff up even before we are aware that we are doing it. It seems natural, even necessary, if we are to make sense of what's happening so that we can formulate a response and create a feeling of security and control. It's very difficult for many of us to simply admit that we don't really know what's happening and to accept the uncertainty that comes from this realization.

How can we stop that habit of making stuff up and still feel secure enough to act based on incomplete information? An answer can be found, surprisingly, in the Bible's story of Noah. Almost every child knows the story, or at least the outline of the story: God is angry at mankind

How often have you seen an event, quickly determined the motives of those involved, passed judgment, and left feeling angry, hurt, or disappointed?

for its lawless and selfish behavior and decides to destroy all life with a great flood, and begin anew. Only Noah, his wife, his sons Cham, Shem, and Yaffet, his daughters-in-law, and two (or seven, depending on the story) of every animal are saved in a huge ark that Noah builds on God's command. This story, though, contains subtleties and messages that are completely lost in this simplified version. There is a disturbing end to this story that most children certainly don't know.

After the waters subside and the ark lands on Mount Ararat, Noah plants an orchard, harvests the grapes, presses them into wine, and gets drunk in his tent. The text doesn't say why Noah gets drunk, or exactly what he is doing in his tent. (As an aside, there is a moving interpretation of this event that sees Noah as experiencing *survivor guilt*. He saw the world destroyed, yet he and his family survived. His drunkenness is his way to dull the pain, terrible guilt, and shame for not doing more to save others.) Then, a strange event occurs. Cham opens Noah's tent and "exposes his father's nakedness" (the Hebrew is not clear on what this exactly means, since later in the Bible, "exposing one's nakedness" refers to sexual relationships). Cham quickly goes out to tell his brothers, who then walk into the tent backwards and cover their father with a blanket.

A strange story, indeed, but how does this relate to MSU? On the surface, we can see that Cham told his brothers something about their father's condition, but the text does not elaborate on the details. The absence in the narrative is revealing, since anything beyond these sketched facts is, by definition, made up. Clearly, Cham told his brothers enough information to lead them to the extraordinary decision to walk in backwards in order to avoid seeing their father in an undignified (or worse) condition. Later, after he awakens, Noah bestows blessings on Shem and Yaffet, while Cham is cursed. So a surface reading teaches that Cham spreads gossip and does not show respect for his father, while conversely, the other brothers refuse to believe Cham's made-up story and are respectful and protective of their father.

There is more to this story, however. A clue is buried in the names of the characters. In Hebrew, *Cham* means "hot," *Shem* means "name," and *Yaffet* means "beauty." These names allude to different human attributes. When someone is "hot," he is in an intensely emotional state; therefore, Cham relates to emotion. A person who has mastered the "name" of things demonstrates intelligence; therefore, Shem relates to mind. The Hebrew root of Yaffet is *yaffeh*, which implies a spiritual beauty. Yaffet, therefore, relates to soul.

The story of Noah, then, can be read as a parable featuring the characters, *Emotion*, *Mind*, and *Soul*—the essential components of our being, housed in our bodies. When faced with a situation that we do not understand, especially one to which we can easily attribute bad intentions, our emotional response (Cham) is usually to make up something, often something very negative. When we stop to coolly evaluate the situation with our intellect (Shem), though, we realize that we don't yet understand what's really happening.

When seen from this perspective, the initial temptation to make something up dissolves. When we further stop and allow our spirit to enter (Yaffet), we see the other person as one who struggles, loves, experiences joy and pain, and wants to do what's right. Just like us. We now see a fellow human being. As in the Noah story, when mind and soul work together, a volatile situation resulting from an emotional reaction can be addressed with skill and compassion.

The lesson of the story of Noah matches exactly the seminar demonstration mentioned earlier. When the young man's "Good morning, Ms. Jones," was not returned, he reacted emotionally and took her lack of response personally, assuming that it was due to her sense of superiority and dismissal of him as worthy of her attention. If he had put that immediate, made-up reaction aside and looked into the situation, he might have learned more about Ms. Jones and may have discovered some useful insight that would help him to develop a positive relationship with her. Now, though, his bitterness will taint any professional relationship he might develop with her. He will be less happy at work, and his career may suffer. All because of something that was completely made up! If we can take this lesson into our lives and work to stop making up stuff—or even better, give the other the benefit of the doubt and assume the best, as we would like to be treated—we then allow situations to develop naturally. Suddenly, we may discover that the person who "snubbed" us is actually a fine individual who is simply overwhelmed at work. Now this person, who we had positioned as an adversary, can become an ally.

Stop making stuff up! This is a tall order and one that I struggle with very often. For me, years of indulging the habit of making stuff up has created an automatic response that feels perfectly natural and expected. The first step in overcoming this habit is to be aware of the pattern and to stop ourselves before we indulge it. Then, when we put aside the immediate emotional response and stop to look with our minds and hearts, we experience the blessing of healthier relationships, we are more open to future opportunities, we are happier, more relaxed and, as the teacher in the business seminar concluded, ultimately, more successful.

WAITING FOR NOBEL

OVERCOMING FEELINGS OF INADEQUACY

Three Jewish mother jokes…

The first is titled, "The Jewish Mother's Haiku":

Is one Nobel Prize

Too much to ask of a child

After all I've done?

The second:

A Jewish man receives a birthday gift from his parents: two sweaters—one blue and one red. The next morning, the door bell rings. The man looks out the window and sees his mother waiting outside. Quickly, he puts on the blue sweater and opens the door.

"Ah, you got the gifts," his mother says.

"Yes," replies the son. "As you can see, I'm wearing one of the sweaters right now."

"So," she says, disappointed, "what's wrong with the red sweater?"

The third:

Question: According to a Jewish mother, when is a fetus viable?

Answer: When it receives its Law Degree.

You don't have to be Jewish to relate to these jokes. These jokes are funny because, like all good humor, they lightly present a dark side of our psyche that we usually have difficulty looking at or speaking about directly. Even though each one features a stereotypical Jewish mother who controls her children through guilt, the Jewish mother is just a convenient scapegoat and lightning rod for a common human condition. The one theme behind all these jokes is our inner suspicion that, no matter what we do, or how hard we try, we will never get it exactly right; that we can never completely relax because we may then disappoint those who rely on us; that we can never let down our guard for fear of exposing uncomfortable sides of ourselves; and that, as these jokes imply, we will never quite measure up because we are simply just not good enough. These jokes are about our unhealthy feelings of shame.

Shame, although it carries negative connotations today, in itself is not inherently destructive. As psychologist and best-selling author John Bradshaw taught, there are two types of shame: unhealthy (which Bradshaw calls "toxic shame") and healthy.

Healthy shame is the realization that, as human beings we have limitations. It is the awareness that, because we are finite, we will inevitably make mistakes but with the knowledge that our humanity also grants us the ability to grow, learn, and change. According to Bradshaw, healthy shame degrades to unhealthy shame when we turn the message, "I have made a mistake" into "I am a mistake;" when the awareness that we have done something wrong becomes the mistaken belief that there is something essentially wrong with us. It occurs when we lose sight of our basic humanness and come to expect that we should be perfect.

For many of us, this unhealthy feeling of shame—that we are, somehow, innately inadequate—seems all too natural. As these jokes imply, perhaps we heard this message when we were children. Bradshaw wrote:

As children [we may have only been] loved for our achievements and our performance, rather than for ourselves. Our true and authentic selves were abandoned.

We may have learned that being just ourselves is not good enough. We may have heard that what matters is what we do, not who we are, and that what we do will never quite meet other's expectations (What, no Nobel Prize yet?).

We may think that this attitude motivates us to achieve, and, in fact, feelings of inadequacy can be a powerful force that pushes many people to strive to reach higher levels. The problem with unhealthy shame, though, is that it is, in the long run, counter-productive. If we believe that we are inherently defective, then we shut off the opportunities to nat-urally learn and grow. When we believe that we are not good enough, we also believe that we must defer to others to receive direction and approval. Ultimately, though, this does not work because no matter how much others may reassure us, no amount of external approval is enough to satisfy that inner doubt. Resolving this feeling that we are not good enough does not get us off the hook from our responsibility to do what is right and to challenge ourselves to achieve and improve. Instead, it liber-ates us to grow in a healthy and authentic direction.

We have all heard sto-ries of people who have attained incredible success yet feel that these achieve-ments are not enough, are undeserved, and perhaps, even, that they are a fail-

The problem with unhealthy shame, though, is that it is, in the long run, counterproductive.

ure. In 1978, Pauline Clance created the now-famil-iar label for this syndrome, "The Imposter Complex." This describes one who, in spite of all the external recognition and acclaim, internally feels undeserving. Such a person, because of this feeling of inadequacy, ends up living inauthentically, detached from his true self and feeling like an imposter.

A recent issue of *Psychology Today* featured an article about clergy who have struggled with their faith. The article included the story of Carlton Pearson, a former Pentecostal bishop who led a mega-church in Tulsa, Oklahoma, with a congregation of over 5,000. In the story, Pearson discussed his growing feelings that the doctrines he had been taught no longer felt true for him, yet he could not allow himself to examine these feelings, out of concern that he would let down his congregation—who expected him to supply ready and comforting answers—and fear that his questioning may eventually lead to abandoning his faith—a possibility that he could not face. Finally, Pearson could no longer live with the pressure of feeling like a hypocrite and abruptly left the church. Looking back, he discovered that his reluctance to question the prepackaged doctrines that he had been given, and fear of examining his assumptions about how a man of faith should act, actually diminished his faith and his sense of purpose. He commented:

> *We spend our lives impersonating who we think others want us to be, and we end up as living impostors.*

Pearson is describing "The Imposter Complex." But he eventually came to a point where he could no longer stand the pain of living inauthentically. Now he is a Unitarian Minister, preaching an inclusive message that matches his deepest held beliefs. His regular congregation is a fraction of what it was, yet he now feels that he is living in accordance with his true self and has a renewed faith and purpose. What matters here is not Pearson's acceptance or rejection of any specific doctrine, but his self-awareness and courage to expose his true self and to accept the consequences.

Like Pearson, how can we overcome our inclination to believe that we are not good enough as we are and live authentically? All of psychology attempts to deal with this issue because this is one of our most essential desires. Spiritual traditions also attempt to offer some guidance. For some people, however, religion itself is a source of the message of unhealthy shame. You might have been taught that religion demands that you be perfect or that there is something irrevocably wrong with you; that your natural desires and ambitions are bad, that your physical nature is innately corrupt, and that you are, at your core, defective. This is *the most* tragic distortion of religion and spirituality.

Although the Bible story of Adam and Eve in the Garden of Eden is often interpreted as a demonstration that we are inherently defective, this story can (and traditionally has been) better be read as a metaphor for the rise of human consciousness; of our unique, God-given, precious ability to choose between right and wrong and to act accordingly. In the story, after eating the fruit of the Tree of the Knowledge of Good and Bad, Adam and Eve are ashamed, cover themselves, and hide. God calls out to Adam, "Where are you?" Of course, this is not a question about physical location. God knows where Adam *is*. The question is a call to humanity to examine our spiritual location. Now that Adam and Eve, as conscious human beings, know of both their limitations and their powers, they are challenged to come out from hiding behind the shame of feeling inadequate and unworthy (being "naked") and stand proudly as themselves—as empowered partners in creation.

An approach to breaking the hold of unhealthy shame that I like very much comes from a deceptively simple Buddhist teaching: *Always maintain only a joyful mind*. This Buddhist motto encourages us to stop taking ourselves so seriously and to give ourselves a break. If you are motivated to do something so significant that you win a Nobel Prize, that's wonderful. But to believe that only then will you finally prove your worth is not only an absurd, unrealistic expectation, it's also not a very enjoyable way to live. The Buddhist nun and author Pema Chodron, in her book *Start Where You Are*, writes:

> *You say to yourself, "I can't do this. I'm hopeless. Everybody else seems to be doing fine, but I don't seem to have any basic goodness." Then you beat yourself up and forget all about gentleness, or if you remember, you say, "You're not gentle! Whack!"... That kind of witness is a bit heavy. So lighten up. Don't make such a big deal. The key to feeling at home with your body, mind, and emotions, to feeling worthy to live on this planet, comes from lightening up.*

In that spirit, a final Jewish mother joke:

> *A group of Jewish mothers gathers together to meet for lunch. The waiter comes over to their table and asks, "Is anything alright?"*

SELF, ACTUALLY

BEING AUTHENTIC

After presenting and sending out the message from the previous chapter, titled, "Waiting for Nobel," I received several emails and phone calls from friends and colleagues who noted that this topic—overcoming unhealthy feelings of shame in order to find our authentic selves—struck a deep chord. "I feel that you must have written that just for me," one friend commented. "I was just struggling with that very issue," another said. The message ended with simple advice on how to respond when we feel that we are not good enough: lighten up and stop taking yourself so seriously (hence, the Jewish Mother jokes). Based on the response from "Waiting for Nobel," this chapter attempts to further explore the nature of authenticity and add some additional, specific ideas on how to address this difficult, but essential, topic.

Authenticity can be defined as:

The degree to which one is true to one's own personality, spirit, or character, despite external pressures and influences.

The idea that we all have an authentic self, unique to each one of us, is actually rather astounding. If you believe that you have an authentic, unique self, then you must also believe that everyone who is alive, or has ever lived, also has this uniqueness. (Other people are unique, too?) Think of it: There are 6.6 billion people on the planet, each with a one-of-a-kind, individual character; each with a specific innate self that is calling to emerge, for a specific purpose; each struggling with the same basic needs and desires, yet each different at the core; each a combination of vast genetic and experiential variables that combine to create a special person. You don't have to be a mystic to find this mind-blowing!

In Act I, scene iii of *Hamlet*, Polonius, an advisor to the king, prepares his son Laertes for travel by reciting a lengthy blessing that includes advice on how to behave well and succeed in a foreign land. Polonius ends the blessing with the famous words:

This above all: to thine own self be true,

And it must follow, as the night the day,

Thou not then be false to any man.

Polonius is telling his son to be authentic—to be true to himself, and that by being true to himself, he will naturally be trustworthy to others. Sounds simple...after all, as the definition of authenticity implies, our true selves already exist. This is why we naturally know when our own authenticity is not being honored; when we are not being true to who we really are. Why, then, as most of us have experienced, is it often so difficult to connect with our own authenticity? The French existentialist writer, Jean-Paul Sartre, alluded to an answer when he wrote:

> *If you seek authenticity for authenticity's sake, you are no longer authentic.*

A true desire for authenticity must be without ulterior motives; without ego or expectation of reward and recognition (a good addition to our growing list of paradoxes). Our desire must be sincere and not for the sake of receiving praise or making a statement. Just because one lives eccentrically, for example, one is not necessarily in an authentic state of being. The eccentricity may be an applied garment designed to draw attention and approval. Beneath may be a shy, thoughtful person who only desires to be part of a caring community. And, of course, the opposite is also true.

A true desire for authenticity must be without ulterior motives; without ego or expectation of reward and recognition.

Michelangelo—who was, for me, the greatest, most powerful artist—taught a deep truth about authenticity in his art. He believed that his purpose was not to *create* a sculpture. Instead, he imagined that he was removing the debris that encased a sculpture, which had always lain hidden in the block of marble. He simply freed it from its confines. Similarly, our authenticity is not created, it is revealed. It emerges when we strip away the veneers of false expectations that we may have placed on it and free the true image below. This is not easy (as anyone who is committed to this process can tell you). It requires tenacity, strength, consciousness, and sensitivity. It requires the willingness to look honestly at ourselves, at the choices we've made, and the beliefs that we've embraced. It requires the courage to remove those beliefs and expectations that do not serve our true selves. This can be painful, but we have to do this because authenticity frees us to be who we are meant to be and to do our life's work. When we are detached from our true self—when we believe that approval comes from outside ourselves—we undermine our self-confidence, leaving us with lower levels of energy, reduced creative productivity, weakened spirit, and blocked intuition and spontaneity.

2,500 years ago, the Greek philosopher, Socrates, famously remarked:

The unexamined life is not worth living.

A twentieth-century psychologist expanded on Socrates' dictum. In 1943, Abraham Maslow published a paper titled, *A Theory of Human Motivation*, in which he proposed a new theory to explain our desire for authenticity. In this theory, Maslow studied extraordinarily creative, productive, and influential people, such as Albert Einstein, Jane Addams, Eleanor Roosevelt, and Frederick Douglass, and determined that human beings progress through what he termed a "Hierarchy of Needs."

Maslow described this hierarchy as a pyramid, with the most basic human needs on the bottom, beginning with the need for food and shelter, followed by the needs for safety, love, community, and esteem. He labeled these basic needs the "Deficiency" or D needs. If these are not met, the individual feels anxious and focuses on getting the missing needs filled. Once the basic D needs are met, one feels secure enough to progress to the "Growth," or G needs. These contain our yearnings to elevate beyond mere survival and begin with the need to engage the mind in learning, followed by the need for beauty, and culminating in the ultimate human need, which Maslow terms "self-actualization." Maslow wrote that self-actualization is:

> *an episode or spurt in which the powers of the person come together in a particularly and intensely enjoyable way, and in which he is more integrated and less split, more open for experience, more idiosyncratic, more perfectly*

expressive or spontaneous, or fully functioning, more creative, more humorous, more ego-tran- scending, more independent of his lower needs, etc. He becomes in these episodes more truly himself, more perfectly actualizing his poten- tialities, closer to the core of his being, more fully human. Not only are these his happiest and most thrilling moments, but they are also moments of greatest maturity, individuation, fulfillment—in a word, his healthiest moments.

At this final level, individuals discover who they truly are. According to Maslow, these people focus on meaning beyond themselves, have a clear percep- tion of reality (including their own strengths and weaknesses), are more concerned with being true to themselves than with the perceptions of others, are growth-oriented, confident—without the need for external approval—philosophically humorous, and creative. Maslow notes that these individuals often have mystic experiences of universal connectedness. This level of self-actualization is identical to the def- inition of authenticity. Of course, not every person follows Maslow's linear path. Artists and musicians, for example, will readily forgo food and shelter in order to create beauty, and one may be filled with self-esteem despite the lack of a loving relationship. The intent of Maslow's pyramid, though, is to iden- tify the steps and guide us along the way.

Last year, I attended a conference in Santa Fe titled "Business and Consciousness." This confer- ence brought together business people from around the globe to discuss the latest thinking on unifying the worlds of work and spirit. World-class speakers led the forums. One of the key-note speakers was Chip Conley, CEO of Joie de Vivre, the largest boutique hotel company in California. In his address, Conley recounted the history of his business. Founded in the 1980s, Joie de Vivre grew steadily until the tech bust of the late '90s dramatically affected the area's economy. Then, the events of 9/11, SARS, and the advent of online hotel booking sites hit Joie de Vivre hard, and Conley was faced with pressures to close his business.

One day, while browsing through a bookstore looking for personal and business help, he noticed Abraham Maslow's book, *Toward a Psychology of Being*. After reading the book Conley was inspired to rebuild his business based on Maslow's Hierarchy of Needs, which he simplified into three levels, relating to the need for financial security, recognition, and meaning. Conley consciously structured Joie de Vivre to meet these needs up and down the pyramid, for his staff, guests, and investors, with a focus on meeting the highest aspiration—meaning. Since then, the company has grown to triple the revenue as before the tech bust, with some of the lowest employee turn-over and highest customer loyalty in the hospitality business. Conley has written a book based on his experiences, titled *Peak: How Great Companies Get Their Mojo From Maslow*. For

Conley, "peak" experiences relate to Maslow's description of self-actualization. Conley writes:

> *I came to realize that creating peak experiences for our employees, customers, and investors fostered peak performance for my company.*

I had the pleasure to speak briefly with Chip after the conference and mentioned to him that I believe Maslow must have been influenced—either consciously or unconsciously—by a passage in the Bible that matches precisely his Hierarchy of Needs. This passage, from The Book of Numbers, is known as *The Priestly Benediction* and is composed of three blessings: the first for physical security, the second for emotional and monetary sustenance, and the third for the highest aspiration of all—the peace that comes from a life dedicated to meaning, aligned with our true nature. These, then, are the ultimate closing words on the subject of authenticity:

> *May God bless you and protect you.*

> *May God's presence shine on you and be gracious to you.*

> *May God's presence turn towards you and grant you peace.*

RETURN THAT CALL

ENLIGHTENED
SELF-INTEREST

A friend and I were recently discussing the moments in our lives when spiritual insight have occurred. We noted that, for us, these moments happened while walking alone in the woods, reading an inspirational book, experiencing the birth of a baby, praying, making love, recovering from an illness, or simply sitting quietly and listening to the small sounds that we typically are too busy to notice. These moments have the power to transform how we view our lives and who we think that we are. At these times, we experience a sense that there are more possibilities than we have imagined and that there is a deeper reality than the one we seem to walk through, and accept, every day. These are profound moments; the times when we get out of our own way long enough to allow something, and someone, else to enter.

Although we might think this type of transformational experience can only occur while we are engaged in "spiritual" activities, like the ones my friend and I discussed, more and more I have come to see these experiences embedded in seemingly mundane, day-to-day events; little insights, lessons, and gifts of wisdom that happen in everyday interactions. One such small incident, which occurred nearly nine years ago, helped me to more fully understand a central spiritual teaching.

This incident was one of those unexpected revelations that happen exactly when one is not looking and occurred in the middle of the work day while I was, in fact, completely focused on the "non-spiritual" activity of trying to develop a new client. In other words, I was in sales mode. At the time, I was working in Charlotte, NC, and was tasked with helping to secure and manage design and construction work in that very busy financial market. One of my targets was a large regional bank that is headquartered in North Carolina. A business acquaintance shared a contact name in the bank's real estate department, and I called, hoping to introduce my company to this potential client. As expected, I got sent to voice mail. *Oh well*, I thought, *what did I expect from a cold call?* So I left a message, with little hope of ever hearing back.

Two hours later, my cell phone rang. It was the person from the bank.

"I'm sorry for missing your call," he said. "How can I help you?"

It is rare that a cold call is ever returned, let alone so quickly, and so, needless to say, I was surprised to receive this call. I briefly introduced myself and described my company and our services.

"You really need to call my colleague who is the Director of Real Estate for the Carolinas," he said. "Here's her phone number…. I'll let her know to expect your call later today."

Now I was beginning to congratulate myself on my expert sales skills. *I must have done or said something that caught their attention. Maybe it's my warm phone voice….*

I followed up later that day and called the number he gave me. The Director's administrative assistant answered the phone. *Okay, the inevitable gatekeeper*, I thought.

"Alan Lurie calling for Ms…," I said, assuming that I'd be asked to leave a message.

"Oh, yes, she is expecting your call. I'll put you right through," she responded. "Hi, Mr. Lurie," the Director said, in a friendly, professional tone. "How can I help you?"

Again, I introduced myself, my company and our services.

"You know what?" she suggested. "Let's set up a meeting with my colleague, our Regional President."

The Regional President! At this point, I began to doubt that this success was due in any way to my expert sales skills or even anything that I did or said (this same basic sales approach never worked so smoothly in the past). I could not yet understand why everyone I spoke with was so prompt and helpful, though.

We quickly set up a meeting.

"We look forward to meeting you," she said.

We meet at the bank's corporate headquarters. The Director and Regional President greet me warmly, bring me coffee, and usher me into a comfortable meeting room.

"How can we help you?" the Regional President says.

By now, I'm getting used to hearing this line and suddenly realize that this helpful attitude must be ingrained in the company.

"First of all, I'd like to let you know how much I appreciate the warm welcome I've received from everyone in your organization," I say, and tell him of my experience with his company.

"Thank you," he says. "It's great to hear that our mission is being lived. After this meeting, can you please send me a note outlining your experience, including the names of the folks you've dealt with? I'd like to send them all thank-you cards."

"Of course. You obviously have an amazing culture, I say, then add, "which is testament to your leadership" *Well, a brownie point couldn't hurt*, I think. *Good sales tactic.*

He frowns slightly, and waves off my awkward, transparent attempt at a personal compliment (so much for my expert sales skills). "Thank you, but it has nothing to do with me," he says, "It's really very simple. We believe in the Golden Rule. Treat others as you would like to be treated. As you know, we also make sales calls to potential clients, hoping to expand our reach and create new contacts. This is how I began in business; making cold calls. Just as we appreciate when people return our calls, we know that people who call us also appreciate—and deserve—a returned call. But," he continues quickly, "we also know that this is good for business. You called us trying to secure work for your company. That's your job. But we also understand that you may be a banking customer. Or hopefully, you may become a customer in the future. Therefore, we treat all calls as though they are from valued customers and future friends."

This was many years ago. Since then, I have told this story dozens of times. Who knows how many folks that I've told have decided to do business with this bank, invest in its stock, pass on this story to others, or just simply feel good about this company? Also who knows how many people have decided to

emulate this bank's model of consideration and concern for others? What I experienced first hand on
that day was the meaning of the Bible's command-
ment, "And you will love your neighbor as yourself,"
and the associated injunction to treat others as you
would like to be treated.

There is a crucial side of this equation that is
often overlooked, however, which was embedded in
this brief experience: To love another as yourself and
to treat others as you would like to be treated
requires that you also love and value *yourself*. You
cannot truly love others and treat them compassion-
ately unless you love and have compassion for yourself, because until this essential internal need is met,
you cannot fully give it to others. Simply put, you
cannot give what you do not have. As the Bible tells
us, when you truly love yourself, you will then naturally love others (hence, the future tense assurance;
"And you *will* love your neighbor..."). Loving yourself is not an end in itself, but is a prerequisite for the
impulse to love others. Self-love in this context is not
narcissism or self-indulgence but is the knowledge
that you, like every other human being, are worthy
of all the gifts that life offers. In this light, interactions
with others are not "zero sum" exchanges, where
you battle for finite resources. Instead, the spiritual
models asserts that (as discussed in Chapter 1,
"Donkey for Sale"), when people engage consciously, abundance flows for all. Through the simple

gesture of politely and promptly returning calls, the folks at this bank in North Carolina acted with compassion for others, while also helping themselves, demonstrating a deliberate policy of "Enlightened Self-Interest." They knew that by treating others as they would like to be treated, they are spreading goodwill while, at the same time, helping their business, which they valued, to grow. This is the ultimate "win-win."

This bank acted with compassion by treating others as they would like to be treated; they are spreading goodwill while, at the same time, helping their business, which they valued, to grow.

Love your neighbor as yourself and treat others as you would like to be treated. Every religious tradition includes this message as a core teaching. These words, though, are not just an ideal that is reserved for special times, locked in religious texts that don't apply to our everyday lives—especially not to the hard world of business. In a very tangible way, I saw these words in action, as practiced by a major financial institution. As this lesson teaches, moments of spiritual insight and growth can occur at any time and often precisely when you are not looking or seeking them. The people I met at the bank consciously try to live the Biblical injunction to love their neighbor as themselves. By acting this way, they help to make the world a kinder place in which to live, if even for that one moment when the phone rings. Here then is a small spiritual exercise that you can practice every day. Return the phone call that you have been avoiding. First, because it is the right thing to do. It's how you would expect to be treated. Even a ten-second message to say, "Thank you for your call," is surprisingly appreciated. Second, who knows?—that person on the other end may someday be able to return the favor, as your colleague, your client, or perhaps as an unexpected friend.

So, a Horse Walks into a Bar...

Taking Time for Laughter

My wife recently sent me an email titled, *Bloopers*. The first part of the e-mail was labeled *History of the World According to Students* and contained a selection of what were described as "actual student answers to history tests collected by teachers." Having been a Sunday School teacher myself, I was interested and glanced at the first selection:

> *Socrates was a famous Greek teacher who went around giving people advice. They killed him. Socrates died from an overdose of wedlock. After his death, his career suffered a dramatic decline.*

"Cute," I thought, as I sat in my office, distracted by paperwork, meetings, and the daily to-do's. I read the next one:

> *Queen Elizabeth was the "Virgin Queen." As a queen, she was a success. When she exposed herself before her troops, they all shouted "hurrah."*

"Now that's funny," I thought, as I chuckled to myself and quickly read the next:

The greatest writer of the Renaissance was William Shakespeare. He was born in the year 1564, supposedly on his birthday. He never made much money and is famous only because of his plays. He wrote tragedies, comedies, and hysterectomies, all in Islamic pentameter. Romeo and Juliet are an example of a heroic couple. Romeo's last wish was to get laid by Juliet. Writing at the same time as Shakespeare was Miguel Cervantes. He wrote Donkey Hote. The next great author was John Milton. Milton wrote Paradise Lost. Then his wife died and he wrote Paradise Regained.

With a wide grin on my face, I read on:

Abraham Lincoln became America's greatest Precedent. Lincoln's mother died in infancy, and he was born in a log cabin which he built with his own hands. Abraham Lincoln freed the slaves by signing the Emasculation Proclamation. On the night of April 14, 1865, Lincoln went to the theater and got shot in his seat by one of the actors in a moving picture show. They believe the assinator was John Wilkes Booth, a supposingly insane actor. This ruined Booth's career.

Now I was laughing loudly. This was really funny! The second part of the email was labeled, *Synagogue Announcement Bloopers*. These were from real synagogue bulletins. The first read:

Thursday at 9, there will be a meeting of the Little Mothers Club. All women wishing to become Little Mothers, please see the rabbi in his private study.

And another:

Don't let worry kill you. Let your synagogue help. Join us for our social after services. Prayer and medication to follow. Remember in prayer the many who are sick of our congregation.

At this point, I had forgotten about the work on my desk, the pressure of the upcoming presentation, and the stresses of the day; I was simply, happily, laughing. These jokes were exactly the type of humor that makes me laugh. Perhaps it is the juxtaposition of a serious subject such as history or religion, with unintentional misspellings, misunderstandings, and confusions that I found so funny. Or perhaps it's just the plain absurdity. Whatever the mechanism, these simple bloopers made me laugh, and I felt happy, in spite of being in the midst of a typically stressful work day.

These jokes may not appeal to your sense of humor; maybe something different makes you laugh. In any case, we all have experienced laughter, and we all know how good a deep, sustained laugh can feel. Whether watching a comedy movie, hearing a good joke, reading something funny, or remembering an event that struck us as humorous, we seem to yearn for laughter—for a good, genuine belly laugh.

What is it about laughter that is so necessary? There have been many philosophical investigations into laughter. In his 1725 treatise, *Thoughts on Laughter*, Francis

We all have experienced laughter, and we all know how good a deep, sustained laugh can feel.

Hutcheson noted that laughter is a response to the perception of incongruity. Such great philosophers as Schopenhauer and Hegel shared almost exactly the same view. We find something funny, they believed, when our expectations and our perceptions do not match. As in the synagogue bulletin, we expect a sober announcement about the good work that this spiritual institution is doing to help young mothers, and are instead given the implication that the Rabbi is the eager cause of these pregnancies. According to these philosophers, it is this incongruity that causes laughter.

Somehow, though, humor resists such dry philosophical explanations. Perhaps E.B. White summed it up best:

Analyzing humor is like dissecting a frog. Few people are interested and the frog dies of it.

To paraphrase the Supreme Court, maybe we can't define humor, but we know it when we see it. We know when something strikes us as genuinely funny because it makes us laugh.

Science has recently begun to study the effects of laughter on the human body, and studies have all come to the same conclusion. Research has shown that laughing can help to:

- Lower blood pressure and increase oxygen intake.
- Reduce stress hormones and release toxins.
- Increase muscle flexion and abdominal strength.
- Boost immune function by raising levels of infection-fighting T-cells, disease-fighting proteins, and B-cells, which produce disease-destroying antibodies.
- Trigger the release of endorphins, the body's natural painkillers, producing a general sense of well-being.

There is now a branch of psychology that has sprung up around laughter. Often called Humor Therapy, this is the therapeutic process that seeks to arouse these beneficial effects of laughter. Humor Therapy originated in 1979 with the publication of Norman Cousins' book *Anatomy of an Illness*, which detailed his experiences in overcoming a serious chronic disease by laughing. While in the hospital and recovering at home, Cousins routinely watched his favorite comedy shows such as *Candid Camera* and Marx Brothers films. Cousins wrote:

I made the joyous discovery that ten minutes of genuine belly laughter had an anesthetic effect and would give me at least two hours of pain-free sleep.

Many major hospitals have now embraced Humor Therapy and routinely employ clowns and comics to visit patients and train the staff. Even the Pentagon, the most serious of governmental institutions, has a laughter program to help relieve stress and improve the performance of its employees. The latest trend in Humor Therapy was created by Dr. Madan Kataria, who has created a practice called *Laughter Yoga*, which combines laughter and yoga breathing. This is taught at "laughter clubs," which bring together groups of people for the sole purpose of laughing together. According to Laughter Yoga's website, there are now 5,000 laughter clubs and studios in more than 50 countries around the world. Many of these clubs meet at workplaces, including Fortune 500 companies, which are embracing both the health and business benefits of laughter—recognizing that a relaxed, happy workforce is more productive, focused, and team-oriented.

Most spiritual traditions have recognized the power of humor and laughter. This may be surprising to some, especially those who view religion as dour and serious, but Buddhism and Hinduism, in particular, espouse the need to laugh, and there is a long tradition of *laughing gurus*, who encourage their students to see humor as an existential human condition. One of the attributes of an enlightened person is a philosophical sense of humor. The Dalai Lama, the leader of Tibetan Buddhism, is famous for his sense of humor and unself-conscious, boyish laugh. Western religions speak of the importance of laughter, as well. The Book of Proverbs (17:22) states:

A cheerful heart does good like a medicine; but a broken spirit makes one sick.

But the final word on laughter must go to Yiddish wisdom that, as usual, is direct, to the point, wise, and funny:

What soap is to the body, laughter is to the soul.

WHAT IF?

FACING FEAR

This chapter was written during the holidays of Rosh Hashanah and Yom Kippur: the Jewish "Days of Awe." At this time, Jews are encouraged to look at themselves as honestly and objectively as possible, to determine where they have fallen short, to seek forgiveness from those whom they have hurt, to fix the damage that they may have caused, and to resolve to improve in the New Year. If this process is truly embraced, then one will stand before his or her Creator in atonement. Judaism is by no means unique in this process. There seems to be a universal acknowledgment that we, as human beings, need a ritualized structure that helps us to commit to personal growth. Every significant religion that I know has a similar process—a way to examine ourselves and to commit to change.

We are all familiar with the idea of New Year's resolutions (as discussed in "In the Beginning"), which serve this function in a secular venue. With all this structure, then, why is change so difficult? Why does it seem so often that all our good intentions and commitments gradually dissolve as we return to the demands of our jobs and the routines of our lives? Of course, there are many possible answers to these questions, depending on the person and the issue that is being addressed. Perhaps we convince ourselves that the changes we committed to were simply high-minded ideals that are not really practical. Perhaps we are too drowned in stress, mired in inertia, stuck in bad habits, blocked by our own pride, or are just too lazy to implement the changes that we know we should make.

There is one essential emotion, though, that typically and ultimately lies beneath the surface of all these reasons. This emotion is so often misunderstood and misapplied that it is difficult to address directly. It is an emotion that resonates deeply for all of us and, according to most psychological and spiritual teaching, is the root of much that ails us as a species. This emotion is fear.

A good general definition of fear that I found in Wikipedia is:

An emotional response to impending danger, that is tied to anxiety. Behavioral theorists have suggested that fear, along with a few

*other basic emotions (e.g., joy and anger), is
innate to higher functioning organisms. Fear is
a survival mechanism, and usually occurs in
response to a specific negative stimulus.*

We feel fear when we are faced with an immi-
nent threat; a hungry leopard lurking in the high
grasses, eyeing us as her dinner, or when we are
approached by someone or something that presents
a real threat to our physical safety. When we are
fearful, we experience specific, physiological reactions: tightness in the chest and throat, oversensitiv-
ity to noise, fast shallow breathing, sweating, loss of
short-term memory, restlessness, twitching in the
arms and legs, and a strange feeling of depersonal-
ization. This is the *fight or flight* response that prepares us to immediately face the danger at hand.

This response worked quite well for our ances-
tor as he prepared to fight for his life, but how does
this emotion serve us today? We may now believe
that fear is no longer needed. In fact, there is a
branch of spiritual teaching that asserts that all fear
is illusion that must be exposed and removed from
our lives. However, when we are truly faced with a
threatening situation that requires intense immediate
reaction, or when we recognize that our actions or
the actions of another can cause serious harm, fear
is a very useful reaction. This is constructive fear. A
person without this type of fear is, in some fundamental way, defective and distant.

We need constructive fear. It calls our attention to real threats and motivates us to action. There is a shadow side to constructive fear, though. Instead of propelling us to action, this type of fear does the opposite and paralyzes us. This is destructive fear.

When we are truly faced with a threatening situation that requires intense immediate reaction...fear is a very useful reaction.

Destructive fear is based on illusory or unactionable threats and provokes an inappropriate, harmful response that comes from mistaking kittens for leopards—mistaking life's inevitable bumps for deadly cliff-edges. Destructive fear is based on "what if" scenarios, in which we imagine terrible possible outcomes to everyday challenges. It is the fear of things that we cannot control and is based upon the mistaken belief that if we are not in control, then we must be in danger. When we live with a sense that life is essentially unsafe, that other people are inherently threatening, and that the world is an irredeemably dangerous place, we experience paralyzing destructive fear.

This is the fear that keeps us from changing because change involves exposing ourselves to the unknown, leaving us uncertain about the outcome, thus provoking fear. And unlike constructive fear, which helps us react to real threats, destructive fear is not effectively actionable and arouses an inappropriate reaction, yet we experience the same physiological and psychological responses as if the threat were real. Because we cannot act effectively from destructive fear, the adrenaline that is pumped in to our system is left unspent, damaging our bodies and spirits and leading to anxiety, stress, and depression.

The first step in overcoming destructive fear is deceptively simple: Acknowledge that it is causing a problem—that it is constricting your choices and keeping you stuck. For many of us, this is a very difficult first step. We may believe that the threats are real and that the changes we had determined to implement present more risk than reward. In this way, we, ironically, become afraid of facing our fear, thereby creating more fear, which makes it even scarier to look at directly. This pattern entrenches our fears and builds an internal defense dialogue that disables us from changing. (*Of course I can't leave this dead-end job, move to a better location, meet someone new, get in shape… What if I can't find anything better? What if I fail? What will my friends, family, boss… think? I could end up with nothing; worse off than I am now. I've tried before, and nothing happened. It actually got worse, and I just made a fool of myself. Besides, it's not so bad after all. Look, people don't really change anyways. That's just some "self-help" nonsense. At least I'm committed and productive; not like those people…)*

It takes courage to identify and acknowledge destructive fear—the courage to face the illusory fear directly, to drop the negativity of our past and the worry that springs from our belief that fear must be avoided and to accept uncertainty. Courage is not *lack* of fear; it is the determination to act *in spite* of fear. Eleanor Roosevelt advised:

> *You gain strength, courage, and confidence by every experience in which you really stop to look fear in the face. You must do the thing which you think you cannot do.*

Dale Carnegie made a similar practical observation:

> *Do the thing you fear to do and keep on doing it… that is the quickest and surest way ever yet discovered to conquer fear.*

Religious traditions offer many paths to addressing destructive fear. As mentioned, Judaism presents a path of self-examination and commitment to change. In Hebrew, the word for fear, *yirah*, also carries the meaning *awe* and the connotation, *to see*. When we feel fear, then, we must remember that the world is filled with the Presence of our Creator—Whose creation is good—and we must accept the responsibility to carefully analyze that which frightens us in order to for us to "see" if the fear is real and valid. Once that determination is made, we can then honestly and courageously choose, free from destructive fear.

Buddhism presents another way to face fear; the path of courageous compassion. Buddhists are encouraged to be mindful of their own fearful reactions and to take note of the things that provoke fear. Those things that cause fear are seen as our greatest teachers because they tell us where we are stuck and where we need to grow. In this light, we see that our fears are not the horrible monsters we imagined, but are gateways to spiritual growth. The Dalai Lama, the leader of Tibetan Buddhism, offers this advice for overcoming destructive fear:

I've found that sincere motivation acts as an antidote to fear and anxiety... the closer one gets to being motivated by altruism, the more fearless one becomes in the face of even extremely anxiety-provoking circumstances.

Christianity presents a path of faith as the remedy to fear. In The Book of Luke, Jesus tells his disciples:

Therefore I tell you, do not worry about your life, what you will eat; or about your body, what you will wear. Life is more than food, and the body more than clothes. Consider the ravens: They do not sow or reap, they have no storeroom or barn; yet God feeds them. And how much more valuable you are than birds! Who of you by worrying can add a single hour to his life? Since you cannot do this very little thing, why do you worry about the rest?

With this arsenal—optimism, altruism, honesty, courage, and faith—we can face even our most daunting fears with a sense of curiosity, adventure, and even fun and discover our hidden strengths and our true purpose.

THE AIM OF EXISTENCE

CULTIVATING HAPPINESS

On a recent trip to Israel, I brought a book to read on the airplane. Because this was a very lengthy flight, I took a book that seemed to promise an easy, light, informative read. My wife, Shirona, had recommended a book, and its title caught my attention. Simply titled *Happier*, this book, by Israeli psychologist Dr. Tal Ben-Shahar, is based on a course that he teaches at Harvard, which is now the University's most popular class, regularly drawing over 850 students. The subject of the class is *Positive Psychology*, a branch of psychology that began in the 1990s and focuses on understanding and encouraging positive human characteristics such as optimism, love, courage, creativity, integrity, and self-knowledge. It is disconcerting to consider that the study of healthy emotions is a new branch of psychology, but since Freud, psychology has typically focused on the negative emotional states—

such as depression, narcissism, personality disorder, and neurosis—that create dysfunctional lives. In comparison, *Positive Psychology* studies the characteristics that lead to fulfillment and happiness.

Although *Positive Psychology* is new, the attempt to understand happiness is an ancient pursuit and is at the heart of most philosophical and religious exploration. The ancient Greek philosopher Aristotle flatly stated:

> *Happiness is the meaning and the purpose of life, the whole aim and end of human existence.*

This is a bold statement that has often been misinterpreted and misapplied. After all, happiness is not easily quantified. Twenty-three hundred years after Aristotle, we still don't have an agreed-upon working definition of happiness, and we still struggle to answer such basic questions as:

- What do we mean by "happiness?"
- Is "happiness" the same as "pleasure" or "gratification" or "joy?"
- What are the causes of happiness?
- How can we find and sustain happiness?
- What is the relationship between individual and communal happiness?
- Can we ever be truly happy in a world of suffering and pain?

Perhaps happiness is such an individual experience that there cannot be any one single definition. Maybe we simply know it when we feel it.

There is a flurry of self-help books that aim to teach quick secrets to obtaining happiness that often include easy techniques (sometimes bordering on the magical) for bringing happiness into our lives. These books usually fail, though, because happiness is not so easily gained. Material possessions, new relationships, new jobs, dream vacations, and even good health may make us feel happy for a short time, but we have learned that physical things cannot make us truly happy. A famous study of 22 people who won major lotteries found that, while immediately elated, all of the lottery winners returned to the same level of happiness as before their windfall, and after a few years they were no happier than 22 matched controls who won nothing.

So if as Aristotle proclaimed, happiness is the aim of human existence, how can we find it? Ben-Shahar provides a systematic process whereby happiness can be cultivated. He begins by describing the four main human archetypal ways to seek and obtain happiness, which he labels as:

1. Rat race
2. Hedonism
3. Nihilism
4. Happiness

Most of us, especially in the West, are very familiar with the rat racer. This person has been taught—by his parents, his school, and his job—to focus his energies on future goals: wealth, fame, prestige. He works hard in school to get good grades so he can get into a good college, so he can get a good job that will lead to a good income, which brings material possessions, respect, and finally happiness. He is told that he must sacrifice pleasure now in service of a larger reward that will someday make him happy. He may even dislike his life at the moment but believes that the sacrifice will pay off in the end. Perhaps he never attains his goals and is left feeling cheated. Or perhaps he does attain his goals but, like the lottery winners, soon discovers that the material possessions he has been seeking do not bring him the happiness that he had expected.

At this point, discovering that the rat race promise of future happiness was an illusion and did not bring real happiness, he may decide that the route to happiness is to seek as much pleasure in the moment as possible. This person, then, moves to the next archetype and embraces hedonism. He now simply pursues momentary happiness, perhaps over-indulging in food, relaxation, physical pleasures, and alcohol. Although all these things are good in moderation, the hedonist soon discovers that, without any goals or purpose, he is still not happy. As John

D. Rockefeller—who was certainly no hedonist—said:

I can think of nothing less pleasurable than a life devoted to pleasure.

Now, having failed to find happiness in the promise of future goals and the short-lived pleasures of the moment, he may decide that happiness is simply not possible. He has tried everything he knows, and he is still not happy. Finally, then, he gives up and becomes a nihilist, feeling crushed by the failures of the past, and convinced that he is a helpless victim of life. He now believes that happiness is a fool's idealistic delusion.

Sounds pretty bleak! We all know such people, though, and most likely at one time or another have even identified ourselves with one of these archetypes. Ben-Shahar points out that these three archetypes don't work because they all focus on only one way to find happiness. The rat racer forgoes pleasure in the present for a future that he believes will bring rewards. The hedonists believe that happiness can only be sustained through ongoing momentary pleasure. The nihilist has come to believe that he has no ability to control his own life and that happiness is an impossible dream.

Ben-Shahar finds a resolution by rejecting these one-dimensional models and embracing a more inclusive, balanced approach. Here, he provides a simple and very useful definition of happiness. He writes:

> *I define happiness as "the overall experience of pleasure and meaning." A happy person enjoys positive emotions while perceiving her life as purposeful. The definition does not pertain to a single moment, but to a generalized aggregate of one's experiences: a person can endure emotional pain at times and still be happy.*

Ben-Shahar titled his book *Happier* because he believes that happiness is not an end; not a destination that one reaches, or a state that one can suddenly pop in to. Instead, we should work to continually increase our level of happiness—to become happier people. We do this when we balance present benefit (pleasure) with future benefit (meaning).

When we look to increase our happiness through work, Ben-Shahar notes that there is one more component that must be added into the happiness equation. In addition to being pleasurable and meaningful, we should also do something that we are good at. The ideal job combines Meaning, Pleasure, and Strength. When we do something that we enjoy, that is meaningful, and that we are good at, we experience the state that psychologists call "flow," when we lose track of time, place, and even self and become completely immersed in our work. These moments are among the most deeply satisfying in our lives, and we are, without goals or agendas, suddenly happier.

In this way, happiness is not an end or a final state that we have earned, but is available at any moment, when we honor our highest potential. As Albert Schweitzer noted:

> *When we do something that we enjoy, that is meaningful, and that we are good at, we experience the state that psychologists call "flow."*

> *Success is not the key to happiness. Happiness is the key to success. If you love what you are doing, you will be successful.*

The simplest advice on happiness comes from Abraham Lincoln, a man who struggled with crushing depression. He discovered that:

> *Most folk are about as happy as they make up their mind to be.*

THE NO NEGATIVITY EVENT

LIVING WITH OPTIMISM

An ad in the *Metro* newspaper recently caught my eye. Among the usual upbeat ads for clothing, restaurants, and movies was the picture of a depressed-looking man, his head tilted, with one hand over his down-turned eyes. Underneath this image was the large letter caption, "The No Negativity Event," followed by a description:

At this Event, we will fight against the negative forces influencing your life! We have helped people in over 90 countries.

Right here in the *Metro*, which boasts that it is "the largest daily newspaper in the world," was this unexpected ad about fighting negativity. This, I thought, is the sign of a good direction toward personal growth. Instead of enticing us to buy more clothing or to see another movie, this ad encourages positive change. This is certainly a much-needed service. Who wants negativity? We all desire good things in our lives, such as health, financial success, meaningful friendships, and committed love. Conversely, we all seek to avoid such negative things as illness, poverty, loneliness, and rejection. This seminar seemed to offer a way to help.

I began to think more about negativity, and wondered: What is negativity exactly? Where does it come from, and how does it enter our lives? One dictionary defines negativity as:

> *Lacking positive or constructive features; gloomy, skeptical, pessimistic.*

Negativity, then, can be linked to pessimism. Next, I looked up pessimism and found this illuminating definition:

> *Pessimism, from the Latin pessimus (worst), denotes a belief that the experienced world is the worst possible. It describes a general belief that things are bad, and tend to become worse; or that looks to the eventual triumph of evil over good; it contrasts with optimism, the contrary belief in the goodness and betterment of things generally.*

Negativity, then, contrasts directly with optimism.

By coincidence (or perhaps by intent), the ad for fighting negativity was printed during the first week of spring, a season of rebirth, renewal, and regrowth, when the cold and stagnation of winter recedes to reveal a new cycle of life. Spring is a season for optimism. It was a quick journey from the unexpected ad for "The No Negativity Event," to the struggle between the opposing viewpoints of optimism versus pessimism. Spiritual traditions clearly stress the need for optimism in our lives and encourage us to discard negativity, and spring is celebrated by most of the world's major religions as a time to develop optimism through the anticipation or commemoration of goodness. Here is a sampling:

- Easter, the Christian Holy Day that celebrates rebirth, redemption, and the possibility of eternal life, occurs in the early spring.
- For Jews, spring is the time for Passover, which recollects the miraculous redemption from slavery to freedom and the promise of a new life filled with limitless potential.
- Muslims celebrate Mawlid al Nabi, the commemoration of the birth and death of Muhammad, the receiver of the Quran.
- Some Buddhists celebrate New Year at this time as well by noting the endless cycle of life, death, and renewal.
- The spring equinox is the New Year for Zoroastrianism, whose adherents believe that good will eventually prevail over evil.
- This is also the most important time for Sikhs, who, in spring, celebrate the birth of their faith.

All these wisdom traditions encourage us to live optimistically and to fight pessimism. Why, then, do we experience so much negativity? Why do so many of us see the negative side of things instead of the positive? There is a saying, which pretends to contain wisdom, that I have often heard quoted about these viewpoints:

A pessimist is what an optimist calls a realist.

This is a pithy and clever quote, to be sure, but is actually a disturbing declaration of a belief in existential negativity, proposing that pessimism is somehow more realistic than optimism. I don't know who wrote it, but this cynical aphorism quickly sums up a familiar attitude—that there is something inherently wrong in the world; that the natural direction of events is essentially toward the worst; perhaps, even, that people are essentially bad, and that given the chance, others will naturally take advantage of you. This saying then relegates the viewpoint of optimism to a delusional, naive state.

Why do so many of us see the negative side of things instead of the positive?

Maybe we have come to believe that this quote is true. Maybe the events of our lives and our understanding of history have driven us to this conclusion. But as the *Metro* ad implies, who wants to live in negativity? Perhaps this is why a "No Negativity Event" is needed—to teach us how to counter this inclination toward pessimism and negativity and how to cultivate optimism.

Let's take a deeper look at optimism. First, is it realistic to be optimistic? Clearly, there is a tremendous amount of pain, suffering, and cruelty in the world. Half the world's population lives in crushing poverty, and unspeakable atrocities occur with all too much regularity. It is staggering to realize that less than one percent of what the world spends every year on weapons could educate every child in the world. Yet, I believe, we live in the best of all times and that things are getting even better. We are living in a time of freedom, potential, prosperity, and spiritual awakening. Ask yourself if there was a time in history in which you'd rather live, and then I challenge you to research the hard reality of existence in that time. You will eagerly return to this time in gratitude and relief. From a statistical data analysis, we can see the positive trends here in the United States:

- Diseases that had previously killed and maimed millions, such as polio, malaria, tuberculosis, and small pox, have been cured. Today, on the average, people live longer and healthier than ever in history. The tragedy, of course, is that this medical prosperity has not been shared with much of the world.
- Women, racial and religious minorities, and others who were systematically discriminated,

oppressed, enslaved, and killed, are now pro-
tected and increasingly integrated.

- Through vast improvements in technology,
  information that was once hidden, unavailable,
  or limited to the elite few, is now readily available to anyone with computer access. Some
  may see this, somehow, as a problem, but it is
  hard to argue that access to information is anything but a good thing.

- Social confines of class, sex, race, and religion
  that once limited one's opportunities have been
  disintegrating, and we are collectively moving
  toward a future where individuals can pursue
  their own dreams based on their content.

- The U.S. government reports the lowest per-
  centage of drug use, especially among young
  people, since such statistics began to be collected in 1979.

- In the U.S., firearm-related crime has plummet-
  ed since 1993, and violent crime is at a two-
  decade low. Most cities are safer than they
  have been in decades (we see this clearly here
  in New York).

- Teenage pregnancies are the lowest reported
  since 1991, with a marked decline in all demo-
  graphics, and more young people, with greater
  diversity, are entering college than ever before.

Science is also pointing to the value of optimism. A long-term study of Harvard University graduates found that those who were categorized as pessimists at age 25 had significantly poorer health or were more likely to have died when they were reassessed 20 to 35 years later. Studies of cancer patients have found that those with optimistic outlooks dramatically outlived their pessimistic counterparts and that the leading indicator for remission is the patient's positive attitude. Other studies have found that optimists are generally healthier, happier, and more successful than those who carry negative attitudes.

This idea, that we should strive to live and act in optimism, and that positive attitude creates positive outcomes, is an ancient one, shared by the world's religions. From Paul, in a letter to the Corinthians, comes the famous words:

> *Whoever sows sparingly will reap sparingly, and whoever sows generously will reap generously.*

The Buddha told his followers:

> *Do not think lightly of good that not the least consequence will come of it. A whole waterpot will fill up from dripping drops of water, so the wise fill themselves with good, just a drop at a time.*

From The Book of Deuteronomy:

I have placed before you life and death, bless-ing and curse. Choose life!

And an extraordinarily similar statement from a Taoist scripture:

Curses and blessings do not come through gates, but people themselves invite their arrival.

These religious teachings encourage us to live in optimism—to see the good and to act with positive intent. This is not to say that we should ignore the inevitable challenges in our lives or turn our back on pain and suffering, bury our heads, close our eyes and ears, and pretend that everything is okay. There is clearly much that is wrong in the world, and one would have to be delusional to believe that there are no dangers, no diseases, and no people who are bent on harming others. What all these traditions teach, though, is that we can, at any moment, make the choice to see the world and the people in it as inher-ently good and to contribute in a positive way. This positive contribution will then increase the good in the world, leading to more optimism. As religion, science, and psychology realize, when we approach a situation with optimism, expecting the best of oth-ers and ourselves, we are much more likely to receive just such a result. By doing so, we improve our attitude, health, and success and actively contribute to humanity's collective growth and our movement toward a glorious future, which is our children's rightful inheritance.

We can, at any moment, make the choice to see the world and the people in it as inherently good, and to contribute in a positive way.

A THANKFULLY SHORT MESSAGE

LIVING WITH GRATITUDE

Last week, I was invited to dinner with a client to celebrate the beginning of construction on her new project. This client invited all the people who participated on her team—the architects, engineers, brokers, project manager, and contractor—to join her and her colleagues after work for a meal together. Over the course of the dinner, the client stood and toasted each person in attendance:

> *"Thank you to Josephine, for your beautiful design."*
>
> *"Thank you to Joe, for your tireless work to find us the perfect space."*
>
> *"Thank you to Oliver, for saving us money and for the good work that we know you will do."*
>
> *"Thank you, Janice, for understanding our needs and communicating them to the team."*

"Thank you to all. Although we may have difficulties ahead of us, I thank you in advance for working together to solve them."

She made sure that all of our drink glasses were full for each of these toasts, and by the end of dinner everyone was relaxed and laughing easily at shared stories and corny jokes.

Such business team meals are not unusual. Sophisticated clients realize that bringing professional people together in a casual environment encourages personal bonding, which will build a stronger, more cohesive, and cooperative team. What was special about this dinner, though, was the client's honest expression of gratitude. She made a point of saying "thank you" to each of us. I felt honored when she singled me out for recognition, and I'm sure that others must have felt something similar. After all, we all like to be appreciated; to receive another's words of gratitude. When someone sincerely says, "Thank you," something in our internal makeup recognizes this as a great gift, and in turn we feel grateful and humbled to be the recipient.

What exactly is gratitude, though? As with all human emotions, psychologists have attempted to define it. One definition that I discovered notes that gratitude is "an emotion that involves indebtedness toward another person," and that this emotion arises when one receives something that meets the following criteria:

- It is valued by the recipient.
- It is costly to the benefactor.
- It is given with positive intention.
- It is given graciously, without any societal or professional obligation.

According to this definition, when these four criteria are met and we allow the emotion to arise, we experience gratitude. This definition is neat and concise and clearly outlines the situation in which gratitude is the appropriate response. The problem with this definition, though, is that it makes gratitude conditional. When one of the criteria is not met—for example, when we don't value the gift or when we don't believe that the gift is costly (monetarily, emotionally, or temporally) to the giver—according to this definition, we are excused from feeling gratitude.

Ethical, religious, and spiritual traditions encourage us to adopt a higher perspective on gratitude. From this point of view, gratitude is something far more profound than a momentary "thank you" for a specific gift. Within many of these traditions, including Judaism, the first prayer that a practitioner says immediately upon awakening is, "I am thankful for having awakened to another day." This feeling of gratitude comes from an existential awareness that our bodies, our minds, our families and friends, the world in all its miraculous diversity, and all that we have are gifts. And that these gifts are given to us unconditionally, at every moment of our lives.

This can be very difficult to incorporate because, as noted earlier, we tend to associate gratitude only with the receipt of a gift that we perceive to be valuable. When bad events inevitably happen in our lives—disappointments, illness, conflicts, deaths of loved ones—we naturally feel bitter and can easily believe that there is nothing to be thankful for. Conversely, when good things happen, we may be tempted to take all the credit and believe that we have achieved these successes solely based on our own efforts and attributes.

At the deepest level of gratitude, though, we can feel grateful not only for our successes, but also for our problems, our faults and mistakes, and even for people who treat us unkindly. We can actually feel gratitude for our most difficult struggles because all of these are seen as somehow beneficial in our lives, even if the intention is not always immediately clear to us.

All religious and spiritual traditions stress the

> *At the deepest level of gratitude, though, we can feel grateful not only for our successes, but also for our problems, our faults and mistakes, and even for people who treat us unkindly.*

essential nature of gratitude and place it as the bedrock of faith. Gratitude is the very basis of our connection to each other and, ultimately, to the Divine. Seen from the highest religious and spiritual perspective, gratitude is the glue that binds us to our true selves and to our highest calling. The greatest human spirits have recognized that unconditional gratitude is one of the most rewarding and transformative practices that we can undertake.

Cicero, the versatile Roman philosopher, stated:

Gratitude is not only the greatest of the virtues, but the parent of all the others.

In a similar vein, the thirteenth-century Christian mystic, Meister Eckhart, advised:

If the only prayer you said your whole life was "thank you," that would suffice.

Psalm 136 sums this up most succinctly, by simply declaring:

Give thanks, because it is good.

And, in her own way, the client who so graciously toasted her team for work done and yet to be done was demonstrating the power of gratitude. From these, we learn that gratitude is available to us at any moment and under any circumstance, even— or especially—when we are not feeling particularly thankful.

The Power of Three

Living with Balance

A person recently came into our office for an interview to fill a senior position. We were very impressed by his credentials, clear presentation, maturity, and personality, so we asked him to send a proposal outlining his employment requirements. A few days later, we received an email with his response. Included in his requirements, along with the usual list of salary, benefits, and other incentives, was a brief description of his request for a "work/life balance" in order to allow for time with family and community.

In retrospect, what was most surprising about this request was that it was not surprising. There is now a growing awareness in the business community that employees are more than mere producers and that people should be allowed the ability to juggle the many demands on their time and attention.

This is a huge and recent change. When I first entered the business world 25 years ago, if I had asked for a *work/life balance*, after my employer had stopped laughing, I probably would have been told: "How's this for work/life balance, buddy? Work more if you want to live!"

We all innately need balance in our lives. In addition to work, we need to focus our attention on our spouses, children, recreation, excursions, hobbies, community, and religious practices. Can we really achieve balance, though? Won't our career suffer; won't we be left in the dust of the more ambitious— the seemingly more focused—competitor? Let's be honest, do we really even want balance? Balance isn't a very exciting concept. Balance is boring. We learn from our culture to celebrate those who have mastered extremes, whether in sports, business, or entertainment. Isn't balance, by its very nature, a concession to mediocrity? Shouldn't we focus on one thing and master it?

The answers to these questions come through a deeper understanding of

> *We all innately need balance in our lives. In addition to work, we need to focus our attention on our spouses, children, recreation, excursions, hobbies, community, and religious practices.*

the nature of true balance. An ancient, profound, and concise statement of the need for balance can be found in a famous quote by the great rabbi known as Simon the Righteous, who lived nearly two thousand years ago. He said:

The world stands on three things, Torah, Prayer, and Acts of Kindness.

These words of Simon seem at first to be very simple, but this simplicity is deceptive. After deeper investigation, we see a glimpse into a universal truth that addresses our very make-up. Simon has distilled a profound truth into one sentence, and there is great wisdom is this short aphorism. Let's examine these three things: "Torah" literally means *teaching* and refers to the need to engage the mind in study; "Prayer" refers to the need to engage the soul through sincere conversation with the Divine; and "Acts of Kindness" refers to the need to engage the body in the helping of others. When I think of Simon's words, I imagine a pyramid—the strongest, most stable simple structure. It is so strong because all parts work in unison to resist pressure. Push on any point or side of a pyramid, and the other points and sides will be engaged to resist and evenly distribute the load. It is very difficult to knock over a pyramid or to deform its shape. According to Simon, it is on this cooperative three-legged structure that the world, itself, stands.

Fortunately, in our very essence, we have been given the capacity to address these three things. To engage our minds, we have been given the gift of the capacity for curiosity. To engage our souls, we have been given the gift of the capacity for faith. To engage our bodies to perform beneficial actions, we have been given the gift of the capacity for compassion. It is curiosity that propels us to study; faith that propels us to pray; and compassion that propels us to perform acts of kindness. What Simon is saying is that we need to activate all three of these centers in order to be complete beings and that our future—in fact, the very continuation of the world—hinges on this balance.

When we fail to achieve this kind of balance, we live below our innate potential and purpose. We have seen the damage caused by "lopsided" attitudes. An excessive focus on the mind (curiosity) can lead to egotism, physical illness, and indifference to others. An excessive focus on prayer (faith) can lead to fanaticism, extreme asceticism, and intolerance. An excessive focus on acts of kindness (compassion) can lead to a loss of self-nurturing, the inability to set healthy boundaries, and a lack of critical judgment. This teaching—that there are three basic components to our inherent nature and that to live fully and meaningfully we must honor all three of these components—is actually found in all spiritual traditions. It is also amazing to see how many other arenas, from the theoretical realm of science and psychology, to the practical realm of business, government, and entertainment, distill their essence to a three-sided structure. Here is a diverse sampling:

Science/Government/Psychology/Philosophy

- The physical universe is based on three irreducible components: space, time, and matter.
- The atom, the basic building block of matter, consists of three forces: electron (the negative force), neutron (the neutral force), and proton (the positive force).
- We live in a three-dimensional reality: right/left, up/down, and forward/backward.
- We experience time in three ways: past, present, and future.
- There are three primary colors, from which all other colors are created: red, blue, and yellow.
- Our bodies contain three primary systems: nervous, circulatory, and skeletal.
- Freud identified three levels of psyche: id (the unconscious), ego (the conscious), and superego (the higher self).
- We have three branches of government that maintain the delicate checks and balances of power: executive, legislative, and judicial.

Religion/Mysticism/Metaphysics

- Christian tradition refers to the Holy Trinity: Father (the Creator), Son (the Redeemer), and Holy Spirit (the Mystery).
- The Buddhist eight-fold path is divided into three essential categories: Wisdom (the path to right knowledge), Virtue (the path to right action), and Concentration (the path to right thought).
- Islam, a religion that fiercely defends God's unity, has three main sects: Sunni (the scholars), Shiite (the traditionalists), and Sufi (the mystics).
- Traditional Hindu belief divides the God-head into three primary manifestations: Brahma (the Creator), Vishnu (the Teacher), and Shiva (the Destroyer).
- There are three Jewish Patriarchs: Abraham—whose attribute is *Mercy*, Isaac—whose attribute is *Strength*, and Jacob—whose attribute is *Truth*.
- Finally, the injunction by Moses to the Children of Israel as they prepare to enter the Promised Land addresses the three components of our being: "And you will love the Lord your God with [1] all your heart, [2] with all your soul, and [3] with all your might."

OK, let's get back to business—literally. This may sound good on paper, but can it be practiced, and what are the consequences? Studies of workers all point to the fact that a person who is given the opportunity to blend work with family and outside personal interests actually performs at a higher level and is more productive and, of course, happier than the person who is not given such flexibility. All forward-thinking companies have programs that allow workers to address all their diverse and often-divergent needs. This may include flex time, work-at-home strategies, or responsibility-sharing with other members of the team. This is simply good for employee retention and a healthy bottom line. We've learned in the hard-nose world of business the importance of balance.

Balance is VERY difficult to achieve (as I write these words, I realize that I haven't called my kids recently to see how college life is going, I haven't been to the gym as often as I'd like, I've done very little charitable work this year, I haven't prayed *sincerely* in too long, I haven't visited my Rabbi is several weeks, I need to follow-up on a few projects, return several calls...), and we all find ourselves pulled to one side of the pyramid at certain periods of our lives; but as all religious traditions recognize, the need for balance is built into the laws of the Universe, and the ability to achieve it is embedded in our inherent human nature. After all, as Simon the

Righteous taught us, nothing less than the future of the world depends upon it.

Post Script

We hired the individual who requested "work/life balance." He has helped teach us, through his example, how to provide exceptional professional services while balancing his commitments to his children, his health, and his personal interests. Thanks Jeff!

Take a Breath

Directed Meditation

[I wrote this paper as part of my rabbinical studies and have included it here to help explain the techniques and benefits of meditation—a popular but often misunderstood practice.]

OK, everyone, please get in a comfortable position; back straight, head slightly tilted downward, hands open on your laps, feet lightly touching the ground. Now, breathe in deeply through your nose. Feel the air enter your body, filling your lungs. Hold the breath for a few seconds, and slowly exhale through your mouth. Breathe in again, and concentrate on your breath as you gently close your eyes....

Does this dialogue sound familiar? Most of us recognize it as the instructions for meditation. You may have personally experienced meditation in a yoga class, at a workshop, retreat, prayer service, or even at a business seminar. If you have not ever meditated, perhaps you may have seen it in a movie or TV show. Or maybe your doctor suggested that you give it a try because meditation is now generally accepted as a valuable means for relaxation and focus. Today, meditation is so common that few people have not been exposed to it in some form. It's startling to realize how quickly this acceptance of meditation has occurred here in the Western world. Just one generation ago, meditation was delegated to the realm of obscure Buddhist/Hindu spirituality, and those who practiced it were often labeled as "New Agers" or as just plain "flakes" (a label I now look back on with fondness).

Now many mainstream Western religions include meditation in prayer services, and most offer meditation classes and workshops. I have participated in many such classes myself, in Jewish, Christian, Buddhist, and Hindu venues, and have led meditation sessions, taught different techniques, and have introduced several forms of meditation in prayer services. I am often asked, though, "Isn't meditation only an Eastern tradition? Haven't we [Western traditions] simply taken a Buddhist or Hindu practice and grafted it on to ours in order to please the current trend?" As a Rabbi, I have even been told directly, "Meditation just isn't Jewish!"

Although many Americans in the '60s, '70s, and '80s were searching for spirituality through alternative paths, including meditation, few knew that meditation is actually a traditional Judeo/Christian practice. The origins of this practice are obscure, but there are numerous references to some sort of meditation in the Bible, and many scholars believe that meditation was practiced during the time when the First (Solomon's) Temple stood in Jerusalem (1,000 BC–586 BC). By the first to second centuries, meditation was so popular that the Talmud notes that over one million Jews were involved in meditation at that time. Early Christianity adopted this practice, and by the Middle Ages, meditation was a well-known technique among the Jewish and Christian philosophers and mystics, as well as Muslim Sufis. We have many texts from that period that specifically address meditation techniques.

Meditation flourished in many European communities until the mid-nineteenth century, when the intellectual pressures of industrialization banished meditative practices to the realm of irrational superstition. After the Dalai Lama fled Tibet in 1959, traditional Buddhist meditation was introduced to the western world. Soon, modern Jewish and Christian scholars and teachers discovered that meditation also has deep roots closer to home, and in 1983, with the publication of *Jewish Meditation*, by Rabbi Aryeh Kaplan (a book that I gratefully acknowledge has informed much of the content in this paper), a deep vein of forgotten meditative tradition was revealed to a Judeo/Christian audience.

Now that meditation is experiencing a renewal, we must ask two basic questions: "What is meditation?" and "Why meditate?" Numerous books and manuals have been devoted to answering the first question, discussing various meditation traditions and techniques. Most meditative techniques, though, are very similar in form and may involve such simple actions as mentioned in the beginning of this paper: sitting quietly, slowly and deliberately breathing in and out, with a concentration on the movement of the breath. Another meditation may include continued chanting of a phrase or sustained focus on an image. Still another may involve slowly repeating a simple activity, such as walking, with careful attention on the details of the activity; knee bending, thigh lifting, body raising, heel touching the ground, toes pushing off for another step....

The second question, "Why meditate?" has varied answers. The physical benefits were already mentioned. Scientific studies have proven that regular meditation provides powerful physical results, including reduced levels of anxiety, lower blood pressure, increased immunity, deeper, more restful sleep, and improved pain management. These benefits alone make meditation a worthwhile practice. Meditation, however, can affect much more than only the body. Meditation can produce a heightened awareness that affects body, mind, emotion, and spirit. Practiced on a regular basis, meditation can

slowly transform the med-
itator, leading to profound
sustained   personal
changes on all levels.

*Meditation can pro-
duce a heightened
awareness that affects
body, mind, emotion,
and spirit.*

So how does the sim-
ple act of sitting, repeating
a phrase or action, breath-
ing and exhaling, produce such results? Most meditative techniques are designed to quiet the mind and
emotions, and slow the body. This process interrupts
the meditator's typical patterns of thought and
response in order to allow the meditator to receive
information and sensations that are usually blocked
by emotions or drowned out by the chatter of the
mind. This is the meditative state.

For those who have never experienced a meditative state, it is somewhat difficult to articulate
because the language that describes it is essentially
metaphorical, like the description of other experiential states such as love, pleasure, or pain. What can
be said, though, is that this is a receptive state,
where the meditator may experience subtler sensations than normally available and access a deeper
sense of self, free from identification with that which
is transient. In this receptive state, change and
growth can more readily occur, whether it is physical healing, the ability to see events, relationships,

and motivations more clearly, or the revelation of spiritual insight and guidance.

To an outside observer, most meditations and meditators may look alike, but the real action is happening inside. It is the meditator's focus that determines the results. This is made clear when we note that the most common word for meditation in Jewish literature is *kavanah**. Although usually translated as "feeling" or "concentration," the root of this word is *kaven*—to aim. Therefore, *kavanah* involves "aiming," or deliberately focusing consciousness toward a certain goal. From this viewpoint, meditation may be defined as "directed consciousness" or "focused mind." In different meditation traditions, these goals vary, from the desire for a healthy body, clarity of mind, or equanimity of emotion.

In most religions, the ultimate goal of meditation is a lofty one; to transcend the limitations of ego in order to create a connection with the Divine. The source of this practice may be traced to the Bible story of Elijah who, asking to see God's presence, sat quietly until he heard the "still, small voice." Aryeh Kaplan eloquently sums up this goal:

> *On the highest level, meditation can provide a person with a personal experience of God. This is certainly the highest spiritual experience. Our experience of God is often clouded by ego and anthropomorphism, so that we tend to see God as a mirror image of ourselves. By freeing*

the mind of these encumbrances, meditation can help us to open our minds totally to the experience of God. In many religious traditions, including Judaism, this is the highest goal of meditation.

Meditation, when practiced with this intention, is a holy activity and can be a partner to prayer, acts of kindness, and study, as a powerful tool for personal growth and transformation. So...

Continue breathing, slowly and deeply. Focus on the breath as it moves in and out. As thoughts and feelings arise, gently let them pass, without judgment, as you return to the breath. Over and over, return your attention to the breath, as it nourishes your body...

*Two other well-known Hebrew terms for meditation are hitbonenut *and* hitbodedut—*literally, "self-knowledge" and "self-isolation." For an in-depth explanation, read* Jewish Meditation, *by Aryeh Kaplan.*

Go Forth

Starting on the Spiritual Journey

[The following is an address that I delivered to a graduating class of Rabbis in 2007. This is included here because the call to spiritual service that applies to clergy and teachers also applies to all who want to live a life of meaning and purpose.]

It's startling to realize that not long ago, I sat where you are now sitting, ready to receive rabbinic ordination. It's startling because I have experienced so many changes since that day; changes that I could not have imagined as I proudly and nervously sat in your chair. Now as I look back, I realize that in a very real sense, a new life began for me on that day. By the end of the day, I was no longer simply a person who, like most of us, raises a family, works hard at his job, and tries to do the right thing—as well as he understands it. Suddenly, I was a spiritual teacher, and with that title came the literally awesome responsibility of living and acting in accordance with that calling.

The fact that you are here today means that you also heard that call and that you consciously answered. You decided to commit yourself to a life of spiritual service, continuing a nearly 4,000 year tradition of dedication, struggle, perseverance, and transformation. According to the Bible, this tradition began with one man, who was the first to hear and respond to the call to holy service. This man was living comfortably with his family in the city of Charan, in modern-day Turkey, when suddenly at the age of 75, he heard the Divine voice:

Go forth, from your land, and from your birth, and from your father's house, to a land that I will show you.

According to the Bible, this lone man immediately packed his belongings, gathered his wife, his nephew, and his followers, and headed for Canaan—Israel. There, he established a new faith that proclaimed that there is one God, Who created us, sustains us, and loves us. Of course, the world knows this lone man as Abraham, father of Judaism, Christianity, and Islam.

This text is somewhat perplexing, though, and several questions quickly arise:

1. First of all, although the first words—*Lech lecha* in Hebrew—are usually translated as "Go forth," they literally can be translated as "Go to/for yourself," since the word *lecha* means

"for" or "to yourself." It seems as though only *Lech* ("Go") would have sufficed. What does this mean?

2. Second, why does the text mention "your land," "your birth," and "your father's house?" Aren't these redundant? What's the difference between these places?

3. Third, why is the destination unspecified? Abraham is asked to go to a land that God will show him, but how can Abraham go to a place before he knows where it is?

4. Finally, can we really believe that Abraham—at the age of 75, comfortably settled in Charan, with family, wealth, and status—would so readily leave?

Because Abraham was, in essence, the first Rabbi—the first man to accept the calling to teach and live in accordance with ethical monotheism—the answers to these questions provide essential insight into the rabbinic journey. Let's look at each question separately:

1. The spiritual journey begins with a dedication to understand and fulfill our purpose in this life and to live in accordance with the Divine will. To do this, we must first look inward to our soul, which is in eternal connection to God. In this way, Abraham's first step was to go

inward, to embark on an internal journey
before embarking on a physical one. The word
lecha, then, carries the imperative to look
inward and to do this for yourself, so you will
be prepared. Like Abraham, you too have
embarked on this internal journey when you
decided, for yourselves, to study to become a
Rabbi.

2. Abraham could not be an effective spiritual
   leader while living in Charan, a land filled with
   cynicism, idolatry, and selfishness. Abraham
   needed to leave that land so that his, and the
   world's, larger destiny could unfold in a new,
   Holy Land. For us, this journey is not necessarily a physical relocation, but a spiritual shift. We
   too need to leave our negative inclinations—
   represented by Charan—behind so that we can
   build a community of morality and faith. This is
   leaving "your land." Next, we must also leave
   behind the specifics of our genetics—"your
   birth." Whether you are short, tall, white,
   black, gay, or straight, your birth characteristics
   do not determine your potential. Like
   Abraham, we must leave these superficial and
   divisive categories behind in order to fully serve
   as a Rabbi. Finally, leaving your "father's house"
   means leaving the limitations of the customs
   and values of your specific culture and having
   the courage to challenge aspects that are not in
   keeping with the higher values that you have

learned and will continue to learn. This can be a very difficult and painful process, but as we see from Abraham's example, it is essential so that we can act purely, free of baggage.

3. I have discovered that as a Rabbi—and a person—I don't really know where I'm going. The road is unfolding in wonderful, challenging, and unexpected ways, and I am learning (with all-too regular resistance) to trust that my path will gradually be revealed over the rest of my life. This is what the text means by "the land that I will show you." The important thing is to get on the road; to make the decision to embark on a committed spiritual path. If you wait to have a crystal-clear idea of exactly what you are meant to do and how you are meant to do it, you will be stuck in paralysis. Just get started with one step. That was my decision and my commitment, as it is yours. There are no assurances, no guarantees, and no promises that the road will be smooth, and you can be sure that you will stumble along the way. Like Abraham, though, we are required to begin the journey with the faith that the way will gradually be revealed.

I don't really know where I'm going. The road is unfolding in wonderful, challenging, and unexpected ways.

4. The fact that you are here answers the last question. When the call to spiritual service is heard and taken to heart, age, comfort, and habit are no barriers. As a matter of fact, Rabbis, like any teachers, are most effective when they have experienced life and when they consciously make the choice to be a guide, regardless of age or social status.

Abraham's journey is the model for answering the spiritual call. As he learned, it is not always an easy journey and is filled with unexpected challenges, set-backs, and vast promise. Like Abraham you have heard and you have answered. Although you may not know exactly where you are going, like Abraham, you will be sustained by the faith that God will show you the way. So, like Abraham, may your journey be filled with joy, growth, abundance, occasional struggle, dedication, faith, and purpose; and like Abraham, may your life be a blessing.

THE LONELY MAN

BALANCING FAITH AND AMBITION

[The following essay was written for the students of a monthly Bible Study class that I lead, which fits in well with this book's theme of finding wholeness.]

There seems to be a paradox at the very essence of our beings. On one hand, we are all discrete entities, separated from each other by our individual physical bodies, our personal histories, our sense of identity, our ideas, specific individual genetic make-up, cultures, and inherent inclinations. In the most literal sense, we are each alone. On the other hand, we are communal creatures, drawn together for survival, commerce, companionship, and love. And when we make a deep connection with another person, we realize that our separation is an illusory surface phenomenon and sense that in some way, our real nature is unity.

Somehow we contain both of these qualities—separation and connection—even though these two qualities appear to be diametrically opposed and call upon conflicting actions: the first requires that we strengthen our sense of individuality and its boundaries, and the other requires that we let go of our egos to allow for a finer, truer self to emerge. We know that some people, by temperament, lean more toward one than the other, but we are all irreducibly both separate and connected.

How can we make sense of this paradox, and is there a purpose or meaning to this observation? The opening chapters of the Bible shed light on these questions. Many people—even avid Bible readers—may not realize that the Book of Genesis contains two different stories of the creation of human beings. The first story outlines the six days of creation, beginning with the explosion of the primordial light on the first day, followed by the creation of oceans, dry land, the heavenly bodies, and all living creatures, and ending with the sanctification of the Sabbath on the seventh day. The second story tells the familiar tale of Adam and Eve in the Garden of Eden, the snake, the forbidden fruit, and the expulsion. These two stories are not conflicting accounts of historical events and are not an error in redaction or a compromise between regional traditions. These stories are, instead, allegorical descriptions of our inherent dual nature. The most comprehensive and cogent exploration of these stories and their meaning can be found in *The Lonely Man of Faith*, written by Joseph Soloveitchik, first published in 1965. This is a very personal book; a masterpiece of self-revelation, philosophy and theology, and is one of the twentieth-century's most insightful reflections on humanity and our purpose here in this world.

Soloveitchik was a complex and controversial figure who lived a traditional religious lifestyle while embracing the modern world of science and philosophy, reaching out to those of all beliefs, and participating in interfaith dialogues.

He occupies a unique and vital position; *a passionate moderate*. He railed against extremism in any form. "All extremism, fanaticism, and obscurantism come from a lack of security," he said, concluding simply, "A person who is secure cannot be an extremist." He was not willing to blindly accept any prepackaged agenda, insisting on finding a path that met his deepest yearnings, and his writings reflect this commitment to find a personal path as he publicly searched for a reasoned and resonant center.

In 1965, he gave a series of lectures in New York City, which were later compiled as *The Lonely Man on Faith*. Soloveitchik sets the tone for the book from the very start with a candid, humble statement.

> *Instead of talking theology, in the didactic sense, eloquently and in balanced sentences, I would like, hesitatingly and haltingly, to confide in you, and to share with you some concerns*

which weigh heavily on my mind and which frequently assume the proportions of an awareness of crisis…. The nature of the dilemma can be stated in a three-word sentence. I am lonely.

He explains that this feeling of loneliness does not stem from being alone. In fact, he notes, he is surrounded by loved ones and close relationships. Rather, Soloveitchik asserts, his loneliness is an existential state of feeling isolated and separate from those around him. "I am lonely," he says, "because in my humble, inadequate way, I am a man of faith." Seeking to understand this condition, Soloveitchik finds clues in the Bible's two accounts of the creation of human beings. The first, from Genesis 1:27-28, reads:

So God created man ["Adam", which has the same root as the words "dirt" and "red"] in God's own image, in the image of God he was created, male and female God created them. And God blessed them and said to them: Be fruitful and multiply, and fill the earth and subdue it, and have dominion over the fish of the sea, over the fowl of the heaven, and over all the beasts which crawl on the earth.

The second story of the creation of man is from Genesis 2:7-8, 2:15:

And the Eternal God formed the man [Adam] of the dust of the ground and breathed into his nostrils the breath of life and man became a living soul. And the Eternal God planted a garden eastward in Eden … And the Eternal God took the man and placed him in the Garden of Eden to serve it and to keep it.

Soloveitchik labels the main character in the first story of creation "Adam I," and the second "Adam II," and notes that there are several major discrepancies between these stories, which can be briefly summarized as follows:

1. Regarding Adam I, the Bible states that he was created "in the image of God" but mentions nothing about the creation of his body, while regarding Adam II, the Bible says that he was fashioned from dust and then God breathed life into him.

2. Adam I is told to "Fill the earth and subdue it," while Adam II is charged to cultivate the garden.

3. In the first account, male and female are created concurrently, while in the second account, Adam is created alone and Eve appears later, created from Adam's "side."

4. The first account refers to God only by the Hebrew name *Elohim*, while the second account also uses the Tetragrammaton, the four-letter sacred, unpronounceable name of God, vocalized as *Adonai* (literally, "My Lord").

Soloveitchik observes that in the first story, Adam I is self-contained, self-directed, and confident. Having been created in "God's image," Adam I aspires to be like his Creator and to "subdue the earth." With his intellect and capacity for technology, Adam I works to control nature and represents the conquest of the human mind over nature; of order over chaos. Adam I is also created simultaneously as both man and woman, so he finds natural comfort in community and does not suffer from feelings of loneliness as he works with others to help conquer nature. Adam I lives in a "majestic community," where he seeks dignity. Soloveitchik writes:

> *Dignity is a social and behavioral category, expressing not an intrinsic existential quality, but a technique of living, a way of impressing society ... Only the man who builds hospitals, discovers therapeutic techniques, and saves lives is blessed with dignity.*

Unlike Adam I, who was commanded to control and manipulate nature, Adam II is placed in the garden "to cultivate it and to keep it." Having been created from the dust of the earth, Adam II is humble and passive. He is a caretaker and gardener, who respects all of creation and recognizes that man is part of nature. In the second creation story, God blew life in to Adam's nostrils, so Adam II has a direct connection to his Creator. Adam II was created alone, without his female counterpart, and he makes his way through life feeling separate. In order for him to have a companion, he must sacrifice part of his very being (his "side"). Community, then, is painful for Adam II. When God observes of Adam II's situation that it is "not good to be alone," Soloveitchik notes that:

> *"To be"* means to be the only one, singular and different, and consequently lonely. For what causes man to be lonely and feel insecure if not the awareness of his uniqueness and exclusiveness?

Adam II's natural state, therefore, is loneliness and discomfort with others, so he seeks to relieve his loneliness through a redemptive relationship with the Divine.

Soloveitchik sees that Adam I can only relate to the Divine through creativity, while Adam II has a "genuine living experience." This is in keeping with the different names used for God in these two accounts. For Adam I, God is called *Elohim*, which, in the Bible, refers to God's attributes of transcendence and creativity. For Adam II, the name *Adonai* is added, which refers to God's attributes of immanence and mercy. Adam I experiences God as distant and unknowable, while for Adam II, God is literally as close as his very breath. Adam I is focused on worldly pursuits and navigates social interactions with ease, while Adam II wrestles with feeling that he is incomplete and cannot engage others easily.

Soloveitchik here identifies with Adam II. His loneliness stems from his feeling of isolation in his struggle to communicate his deepest spiritual yearnings to a world that seems to idolize its own power and intellect; a world dominated by Adam I's attributes of creativity and control.

Here, Soloveitchik discovers one of the great lessons from the two creation stories: They are descriptions of the two major inherent characteristics of human beings.

> *Adam the first, majestic man of dominion and success, and Adam the second, the lonely man of faith, obedience, and defeat, are not two different people locked in an external confrontation, but one person who is involved in self-confrontation. ...In every one of us abide two personae—the creative majestic Adam the first, and the submissive, humble Adam the second.*

Although most of us are created with a natural affinity for one for the other, both of these aspects are essential in order to be fully human, and each of us needs to recognize, embrace, and integrate these apparent opposites of our nature. A crisis between these two aspects of humanity occurs when the attributes of Adam I are not balanced by Adam II; when our urge to create and dominate pushes aside our ability to experience humility, gratitude, and faith. We have all experienced this phenomenon; when our rational, scientific mind, with its need to understand and control, overwhelms our subtler faculties. In those moments, we come to believe that all our accomplishments are only a result of our own efforts and forget that our lives are intertwined with others and that we are sustained by an unending gracious Source. The result is arrogance and insensitivity. On the other hand, we have been given a mind and a body to physically accomplish what is needed and to live in supportive community. To retreat into spiritual isolation and live only to explore individual mystical experiences is equally self-centered and is an abdication of our responsibilities to others.

There are those involved in religion, for example, who find in it only the mastery of tradition and ritual and the reinforcement by a loose community of like-minded people. For these people, faith has been covered by the thin topsoil of the form of religion, until the notion of true faith—a desire to connect to the Divine—is completely hidden. Conversely, though, faith needs a vessel, a form, and a practice because faith without action is also incomplete.

One part of us knows action; another knows prayer. We need both. The reconciliation of these opposites comes with conscious attention. We must balance the will to subdue with the humility of loneliness. We must walk confidently and honor our intellect, while bending in gratitude and humility to that which we cannot rationally comprehend. We must respect our bodies and our own needs, while recognizing that everyone and everything is eternally connected to, and a product of, the same Source.

As the Bible notes, it is not good to be alone, and in the integration of these two inherent natures, we find wholeness.

We must balance the will to subdue with the humility of loneliness.

WHAT'S IN YOUR POCKET?

INTEGRATING OPPOSITES

I have recently been rereading the weekly messages from the last twelve months in preparation for compiling a selection of them into this book. As I was working to arrange them, I noticed one consistent theme that continued to emerge. This theme seemed to underlie the content and direction of all the weekly messages, whether the subject was conflict of interest, happiness, persistence, or ethical wealth. Perhaps this is because this theme is one that resonates for me, or perhaps this is some sort of bedrock teaching, or perhaps I'm just not very versatile. Whatever the case, the one theme that consistently runs through all the weekly messages is this: the need to struggle to see beyond easy, packaged answers and to avoid "either/or" thinking; to embrace apparent opposites and become comfortable with paradox. In the language of philosophy and theology, this theme, simply stated, is the rejection of dualistic thinking.

Dualism refers to the belief that the world is essentially composed of two opposite, battling forces: good vs. evil, right vs. wrong, physical vs. spiritual, mind vs. spirit, order vs. chaos, security vs. freedom, justice vs. compassion, doer vs. thinker, serious vs. frivolous, religious vs. scientific, faith vs. doubt, spiritual vs. realistic, us vs. them, me vs. you. Many philosophical and religious traditions utterly reject dualism, which, they argue, is an illusory, erroneous, and dangerous world view that, because it is based on faulty assumptions, inevitably leads to disastrous results.

The one theme that consistently runs through all the weekly messages is this: the need to struggle to see beyond easy, packaged answers, and to avoid "either/or" thinking; to embrace apparent opposites.

Dualism is a simplistic way of thinking that allows us to believe that there is one exclusive avenue to absolute truth to which we can subscribe, and that those who disagree—or that which contradicts—this truth are absolutely wrong. When we divide our reality into two opposing camps, we immediately set up a confrontation with no resolution except the conversion or destruction of one of them. In mystic traditions such as Zen and Kaballah, the cause of all our suffering is this dualistic thinking, stemming from our attachment to shifting transient forms and our fear of discovering who we really are. A dualistic mind is intolerant of anyone or anything that differs from its claim to truth and sees one who disagrees as ignorant or as a dangerous adversary. A mature mind, these spiritual traditions teach, is comfortable with contradictions, accepts that there is much that we simply cannot know, and sees paradoxes as avenues to higher, unified truths. As my teacher, Rabbi Joseph Gelberman, often advises:

> Never say, "Instead of." Always say, "In addition to."

The philosophical solution to dualism is found through a method known as "dialectic." Dialectic thinking requires that we openly examine both sides of an issue until a synthesis is found that integrates views from both to find a higher truth that fuses the opposites. This fusion of opposites seems to be built into nature. Quantum

When we divide our reality into two opposing camps, we immediately set up a confrontation with no resolution except the conversion or destruction of one of them.

physics has demonstrated that electrons are some-how both physical (particles) and non-physical (waves) at the same time. The resolution is the the-ory that matter exists only in a potential state until an observer participates. A more accessible, experi-ential example is the fact that we reconcile opposites at every moment of our lives, with every thought. Our brains, which are composed of physical matter, somehow produce a non-physical product called thoughts. The synthesis of these opposites is the understanding that our minds are the unity of matter and non-matter, animated by the primordial flow of consciousness that enters our bodies.

A good example of unifying opposites comes from Herb Elliot, who was the world record holder in the mile run from 1958 to 1962. Mr. Elliot had this to say about what it takes to achieve at that level:

> *To be a world-record holder in the mile, a man must have the arrogance it takes to believe he can run faster than anyone ever has at the dis-tance; and the humility it takes to actually do it.*

We typically think of arrogance and humility as opposites, and most of us believe that arrogance must be tamed to develop humility. Yet, there are times when healthy arrogance—which can be defined as the belief that, in a particular area, you are more knowledgeable, capable, or skilled than others—is needed; when you should forcefully fol-low your own agenda. As Henry Ford said:

If I had asked my customers what they wanted, they would have said a faster horse.

And, of course, there are times when true humility—the knowledge that we are all limited and finite—is called for. Einstein, who penetrated deeper into the workings of the Universe than any other human being, and who certainly had the right to be arrogant, said:

What separates me from most so-called atheists is a feeling of utter humility toward the unattainable secrets of the harmony of the cosmos.

Einstein thought that those who view the vastness of the Universe only through the narrow lenses of their own intellects, have become so rigid that "they cannot hear the music of the spheres." The pride in their intellect cut them off from experiencing the beauty and power—and, hence, the real nature—of the very object that they are studying.

Elliot noted that arrogance and humility are both qualities that can be harnessed toward a common, purposeful goal. We know, though, that these qualities are usually not so simple. Often, the appearance of arrogance is developed in order to hide uncomfortable feelings of shame and insecurity, and humility may be a false front to cover a raging ego.

In the same way, faith may be a shield to avoid looking at our doubts, bigotry may be a means for deflecting one's sense of inadequacy, and skepticism may be a fabricated tough front to protect someone who is inherently trusting but is afraid to bestow that trust. In this way, we see that these apparent opposites may simply be defense mechanisms to protect a part of us from which we feel vulnerable. The resolution is in having the awareness to become conscious of this dynamic and the courage to expose your true self. Then, the "opposites" can be seen simply as construction pieces of the same object, which has been built to defensively obscure the reality below.

A great aphorism that teaches us how to implement these opposite sides of our make-up comes from *The Sayings of the Fathers*, a book of ethical dialogue from the Talmud that I often quote. Hillel, the great liberal Rabbi, who lived in the first century, famously said:

> *If I am not for myself, who is for me?*
>
> *When I am only for myself, what am I?*
>
> *If not now, when?*

Hillel teaches that we have the obligation to balance our personal needs, goals, ambitions, and desires with those of others. This is not an "either/or" paradigm; we are not either selfish or altruistic. We are both, and we need both. First, we must look after our own needs. We cannot delegate or abdicate the responsibility to take care of our health, earn a living, raise a family, and enjoy the pleasures that life offers. On the other hand, if that is all we do—if our only focus is on ourselves—we are not a conscious, moral, engaged, human being. Hillel ends by saying that this is not some abstract idealistic theology, but is something that we can, and must, implement right now. The entry point exists in the present, each time we decide. He phrases his aphorism in the form of questions because we are meant to continually question ourselves and to honestly ask if we are properly aligned.

Before I am about to speak in public—and am getting nervous or anxious—I often remember a favorite story about reconciling opposites and using both appropriately. There was a young man, the story tells, who was asked to deliver an important speech to his peers and public. This was his first opportunity to present his ideas, and he was eager to impress. As he sits, waiting to be called up, he looks at the crowd. Recalling the motivational tapes he's been listening to in preparation, he thinks,

> *They are going to be blown away by me. After this speech, my career will take off. They won't know what hit 'em!*

He hears his name announced, stands up straight, and walks proudly to the podium. As his foot reaches the last step, he slips, drops his papers, and catches himself on the rail. He bends over to pick up his papers and tries to regain his composure. But as he reaches the lectern, he looks out to the crowd, sees their concerned expressions, and blushes. Now, sweating and flushed from having revealed his awkwardness, he hesitantly clears his throat, wipes his forehead, and, voice shaking, stumbles through the presentation. Head down, he walks humbly back to his seat, as the audience politely applauds.

Afterwards, he sees a friend—an older man—at the reception. The older man puts his hand on the younger man's shoulder and says,

"If you had gone up the way you went down, you would have gone down the way you went up."

In other words, if he had gone up to give his speech with a feeling of humility—with gratitude for the opportunity to speak, the awareness that there are many listening who know more than he, and the recognition that he is just at the beginning of his career—he would have connected with himself, his material, and his audience, in a healthy, meaningful way and would have come down afterwards with an earned feeling of pride and accomplishment and the energy from a real interaction with his audience. Instead, in his misplaced eagerness to impress, he actually accomplished just the opposite.

There is a wonderful teaching that helps to understand this dynamic. Rabbi Bunam, a nineteenth-century Chasidic master, told his disciples:

Every person should carry two small inscribed stones; one in each pocket. In the right pocket should be the words, "For my sake the world was created." In the left pocket should be the words "I am but dust and ashes."

Bunam's teaching is similar to mile-runner Herb Elliot's remark. We need both aspects of our nature: healthy arrogance and true humility. When we practice this difficult but essential balance, we begin to see that the world is at once both more complex and more simple than we had imagined. We can be open to new experiences and ideas and can accept ourselves and others as we are. We can put aside our impulse to categorize, judge and separate, and will embrace difficulties with the confidence of uncertainty. We will then accept success with the humility that comes from the knowledge of our own inherent worthiness. At times, when we are feeling insecure, unworthy, and unloved, we can remember that we are created in God's image, connected to the Divine and that all the world's blessings have truly been created just for each of us. When we are feeling superior, aloof, and self-absorbed, we can remember that we are physical creatures, that our time on Earth is limited, and that from the highest possible perspective, we are all equal in God's sight.

INDEX

Index

Press

FINANCIAL TIMES

In an increasingly competitive world, it is quality
of thinking that gives an edge—an idea that opens new
doors, a technique that solves a problem, or an insight
that simply helps make sense of it all.

We work with leading authors in the various arenas
of business and finance to bring cutting-edge thinking
and best-learning practices to a global market.

It is our goal to create world-class print publications
and electronic products that give readers
knowledge and understanding that can then be
applied, whether studying or at work.

To find out more about our business
products, you can visit us at www.ftpress.com.